catching
readers

grade **3**

THE RESEARCH-INFORMED CLASSROOM SERIES

Consider daily life for a child struggling with reading. Imagine what it is like to go through school day after day feeling that you are bad at the one thing that school seems to value most. Imagine struggling with everything from independent reading to reading directions on a math worksheet. Imagine what that feels like. . . .

While there are all sorts of pressures to improve instruction for struggling readers—to raise test scores, to make adequate yearly progress (AYP), and so on—the most compelling reason is to help as many children as possible avoid that feeling. We want to enable children to go through elementary school feeling, and being, successful.

Barbara Taylor brings decades of research and development to the question of how to help struggling readers become successful. *Catching Readers: Grade 3*, which is part of the Early Intervention in Reading series, brings the resulting insights to you, in the form of concrete and specific practices that have been shown to help children who struggle improve their reading. These books could not come at a more important time, as response to intervention (RTI) leads schools to invest more than ever in small-group reading instruction. The multifaceted and responsive teaching at the heart of the approach Taylor describes is a welcome contrast to the myopic, scripted programs marketed so heavily under the banner of RTI.

These books exemplify the ideals of the Research-Informed Classroom series—bringing rigorous classroom-based research to bear on persistent challenges of classroom practice. This series aims to bridge the gap between research and practice by focusing on the most practical, classroom-relevant research and communicating practices based on that research in a way that makes them accessible, appealing, and actionable. The series is founded on the belief that students and teachers are researchers' clients, and serving them should be the highest priority.

As with so much of the best educational research and development, Taylor has collaborated extensively with teachers close to home and throughout the United States. Indeed, one might say we've gone full circle, from Teacher-Informed Research to Research-Informed Teaching. So thank you, teachers, and thank you, Barbara, for this important contribution to reading success for all children.

—*Nell K. Duke*

MICHIGAN STATE UNIVERSITY

catching
readers

grade 3

DAY-BY-DAY SMALL-GROUP READING INTERVENTIONS

Barbara M. Taylor

HEINEMANN
Portsmouth, NH

Heinemann
361 Hanover Street
Portsmouth, NH 03801–3912
www.heinemann.com

Offices and agents throughout the world

The author and publisher wish to thank those who have generously given permission to reprint borrowed material in this book and/or on the DVD:

Cover art and excerpt from *George and Martha Tons of Fun* by James Marshall. Copyright © 1980 by James Marshall. Published by Houghton Mifflin Company. Used by permission of the publisher.

Cover art from *The Outside Dog* (I Can Read Books: Level 3) by Charlotte Pomerantz, illustrated by Jennifer Plecas. Text copyright © 1993 by Charlotte Pomerantz. Illustrations copyright © 1993 by Jennifer Plecas. Used by permission of HarperCollins Publishers.

Library of Congress Cataloging-in-Publication Data
Taylor, Barbara M.
    Catching readers, grade 3 : day-by-day small-group reading interventions / Barbara M. Taylor.
        p. cm.—(Early intervention in reading series) (The research-informed classroom series)
    Includes bibliographical references.
    ISBN-13: 978-0-325-02890-3
    ISBN-10: 0-325-02890-7
    1. Reading—Remedial teaching. 2. Individualized instruction. I. Title. II. Title: Catching readers, grade three.
    LB1050.5.T335 2010
    372.43—dc22
                                  2010010286

Editor: Wendy Murray
Production editor: Patricia Adams
Video editor: Sherry Day
Video producer: Bob Schuster, Real Productions
Cover design: Lisa Fowler
Typesetter: Gina Poirier Design
Manufacturing: Valerie Cooper

Printed in the United States of America on acid-free paper
14   13   12   11   10   ML   1   2   3   4   5

This book is dedicated to the many third-grade teachers who work tirelessly to provide motivating instruction that meets their students' needs, challenges them all, and is instrumental to their success in reading.

Contents

1 Helping Third Graders Who Struggle
Lessons That Sit Within Effective Reading Instruction · **1**

2 Meet the Teachers
The Differentiated Lessons and Teacher Collaboration That Support EIR · **14**

The Five-Day Lesson Routine 27

Additional Instructional Strategies 59

Assessing Third Graders in EIR 69

Managing Your Reading Block with EIR 81

On the DVD

 Downloadable Classroom Reproducibles

    Over 100 pages of full-size forms and teaching resources.

Teaching Resources on the DVD

Chapter 5

Chapter 6

Chapter 7

Foreword

I began my teaching career as a first-grade teacher in Key West, Florida, in 1965. Much has changed since then in the world and in the world of school. But reading Barbara Taylor's books made me realize how much is still the same. My class of thirty-five children contained nine children—two girls and seven boys—who were (in the lingo of the day) "not ready." In those days, basal reading series for first grade had a readiness book that I was very grateful to find. I grouped these nine students together and we made our way through the workbook pages. The pages were mostly practice with letter names and auditory discrimination—the precursor of phonemic awareness. Six weeks into the school year, we finished the readiness book and I administered the Metropolitan Readiness Test to my students. For three days, I tried to keep them focused on the correct lines and asked them to underline the letter *b*, put an *x* on the picture that began like *paint,* and circle the picture of the object that rhymed with *cat.* I took all these booklets home and spent a miserable weekend grading them. As I made my way through the test booklets, I adopted a "benefit of the doubt" scoring system. "Two red marks on this line, none on the next. If the second mark is on the next line, it would be right. I'm counting it correct." In spite of my lenient scoring, scores for eight of the nine children indicated they were still "not ready." I spent a sleepless Sunday night wondering what I was to do with these children who were clearly not ready when I had used up all the readiness materials! Lacking any alternative, I started them in the first pre-primer and we plodded our way through the books. By the end of the year, only one of these students could read fluently at primer level.

If Barbara had written her books 45 years earlier (when she was probably in kindergarten), I think I could have transformed my "not ready" kids into fluent readers. Based on many years of research in real classrooms with real teachers and kids, Barbara has created a workable system for providing struggling readers in grades K–5 with the targeted intervention they need to become fluent readers. At the heart of Early Intervention in Reading (EIR) is the addition of a second reading lesson in a small-group setting. Unlike many interventions, struggling readers get this second reading lesson *in addition to* all the rich classroom instruction and *in* the classroom—not in some room down the hall. With details, specifics, and examples that only someone who has spent many hours in the classroom could know, Barbara guides you step-by-step as you organize for and provide effective EIR instruction. As you read through the book, your brain races with questions:

- "How do I fit an additional intervention group lesson into my daily schedule?"

- "What books work best for these lessons?"

- "How can I provide all the instruction struggling readers need in 20 minutes?"

- "What does the coaching for decoding and comprehension look like and sound like?"

- "How do I wean them off my coaching and move them toward independence?"

- "How do I provide worthwhile independent activities for the students I am not working with?"

Because Barbara has worked in many so classrooms coaching teachers who are implementing EIR, she can provide practical, classroom-tested answers to all your questions. She invites you into the classrooms of real teachers and you get to hear them describing how they organize and problem solve. In addition to the printed resource, you can go to the video clips on the DVD to "See It in Action." As you watch real teachers move through the three-day lesson sequence, you realize that, while it is complex, Barbara provides all the resources you need to make it work in your classrooms with your students who struggle.

Once you see how EIR works in your classroom, you will probably want to spread the word. Not to worry! Barbara is right there supporting you. In the final chapter, "Creating an EIR Community," she provides a detailed, month-by-month plan for organizing a group of colleagues to learn together how to better meet the needs of struggling readers.

So, if they ever invent a time machine that could transport me back to 1965, with the help of Barbara Taylor's books, I know I could teach all my "not ready" kids to read!

Patricia M. Cunningham
Wake Forest University

Acknowledgments

This book is the result of fifteen years of collaboration with many third-grade teachers and colleagues across the United States. I want to thank them all for their invaluable contributions to this book.

Inspired by Reading Recovery, I developed the Early Intervention in Reading (EIR) process in the late 1980s to help first-grade teachers help their at-risk readers succeed in reading through daily, small-group, reading intervention lessons. I have refined the EIR process over the years by visiting many classrooms and learning from many teachers and their students. Without this opportunity, I would not have been able to modify and improve the EIR teaching strategies and professional learning practices described in this book.

I also want to thank the hundreds of third-grade teachers I have visited and learned from over the past ten years through my work on effective reading instruction and schoolwide reading improvement. I especially want to thank the exemplary teachers who have contributed so much to the book by sharing their thoughts and lessons related to effective reading instruction.

I owe a special thanks and a debt of gratitude to my colleague, Ceil Critchely, a master teacher who has been instrumental in helping teachers succeed with EIR through the phenomenal professional learning support she has provided to them over the past twelve years. I know that without Ceil's expert guidance, teachers would not have been as successful as they have been in helping their at-risk readers learn to read well by the end of third grade.

I also want to thank my academic colleagues for their support and feedback. In particular, I want to recognize my good friends, Kathy Au and Taffy Raphael, who have gently nudged me over the years to publish my work on EIR in a form readily accessible to teachers.

I want to thank the many people at Heinemann who have made this book possible. Thanks to Wendy Murray, my editor, who saw how this book could support teachers with an instructional process to help their at-risk readers succeed in reading. She has done a remarkable job cutting unnecessary sentences and paragraphs, adding teacher-friendly phrases, reorganizing entire sections, and designing the book so it is easy for teachers to read and to follow. I also want to thank Patty Adams, my production editor, for her top-notch work on a complex project within a challenging time frame. Whenever I called with questions or concerns, she responded cheerfully and promptly. Many others at Heinemann have also contributed to this book and I thank them for their efforts.

It is my sincere hope that third-grade teachers will find this book useful as they strive to teach students who come to them a little behind in the fall to be confident, successful, readers by the end of the school year. Thanks to all third-grade teachers reading this book for the important work you do for our children!

Barbara M. Taylor
University of Minnesota

Introduction

We are a culture of quick fixes. We promise mastery in ten easy lessons, instant success, overnight sensations. Go to a bookstore and whether you stand and gaze at the brightly colored covers in the business, health, or education section, the answer to our every need is couched in words like *speedy, easy,* and *seven easy steps.*

In such a culture, a lot of alarm bells go off when a teacher faces an eight-year-old child in third grade who is behind in learning to read. *Catching Readers, Grade 3,* is one book in a series of five, dedicated to giving the regular classroom teacher what's needed to reach and teach that eight-year-old with a concrete plan rather than a frantic pull-out program or a misguided label. Each book in the series offers teacher-friendly, research-proven background and lessons for young readers who need an extra boost.

The intervention model brings reading success to children in a five-day lesson cycle, which I know sounds as though I'm playing into the same glib promises of swift solutions. I state it here as a way to express that it is a five-day format used across a school year with deep roots—more than fifteen years of classroom testing. I emphasize the "five-day" repetition of the lessons to make it clear that we don't have to choose to run around in circles looking for some new complicated program for reaching at-risk readers. We know what to do. When we're true to children's developmental levels, know which books to put in their hands, and provide effective instruction, a lot of good things fall into place. The key is to focus on the children and the practices we know help them to read at each grade level.

In fact, the intervention model I offer stands in opposition to approaches and programs that think the answer to helping K–5 below-grade-level readers achieve is to provide remediation. Above-grade-level, on-grade-level, and below-grade-level readers all need the same thing: sound teaching techniques and developmentally appropriate practices that meet their needs and provide intellectual challenge to all.

Here's an overview of how the interventions are unique and yet similar for each grade level, so you can see the developmentally based, purposeful overlap in the series. The intervention gives teachers, staff developers, principals, and reading coaches a predictable model so that schoolwide coherence is easier to attain. All grade-level models stress word-recognition proficiency, high-level comprehension, vocabulary development, and strategic reading. Unique components of the various grade-specific models are described below:

Kindergarten

The daily 10-minute supplemental lessons for kindergarten focus on developing all children's oral language, phonemic awareness, and emergent literacy abilities through literature-based activities. The goal is for all students to leave kindergarten with the skills they need to learn to read in first grade. The more capable children, as they respond to the various activities in EIR lessons, serve as models for the children who are less skilled in oral language and emergent literacy abilities. Less-skilled children who need more support return to some of the story discussion questions and phonemic awareness/emergent literacy activities for an additional 10 minutes a day.

First Grade

First-grade children who start the school year with lower-than-average phonemic awareness abilities and letter-sound knowledge will benefit from EIR lessons. The teacher focuses on accelerating students' literacy learning by deliberately coaching them to use strategies to decode words as they read, to actively engage in word work, and to think at a higher level about the meaning of the texts they are reading.

Second Grade

Second-grade readers who can't read a book at a first-grade level at the start of second grade will benefit from the basic EIR routine. The intervention begins with first-grade books and routines of the grade 1 EIR model and then moves into second-grade books a few months later. There is also an accelerated grade 2 routine designed for students who come to second grade as independent readers but who will need additional support to be reading on grade level by the end of the school year.

Third Grade

The grade 3 EIR routine is for children who are reading below grade level when they enter third grade. In the grade 3 EIR model, the focus is on refining students' decoding of multisyllabic words, improving their fluency, developing their vocabulary, and enhancing their comprehension of narrative and informational texts. Ideally, the grade 3 EIR model is done within the context of a cross-age tutoring program in which the third-grade students read to and also tutor first-grade EIR students. The third graders are working on their reading for more than "catching up because they are behind." They look forward to and enjoy working with their younger student who needs additional support in reading.

Fourth/Fifth Grade

The EIR routine for fourth and fifth grade is for children who are reading below grade level at the beginning of the school year. Although students receive support in attacking multisyllabic words and developing reading fluency, the grade 4/5 model focuses on improving students' comprehension of informational text through the use of comprehension strategies, discussion of vocabulary, and engagement in high-level talk and writing about texts. Ideally, the grade 4/5 EIR model is done within the context of a motivating cross-age tutoring program in which fourth and fifth graders read to and also tutor second or third graders.

Getting Good at It: Different Ways to Use This Book

This book—and by extension all the books in this series—is designed to be used by the individual teacher, a pair or group of teachers, or as part of a schoolwide professional development plan. Here are components that support collaborative learning:

Video Clips for Individual Viewing

As you read about the recurring cycle of EIR routines, I encourage you to watch the video clips that illustrate what is being covered in the text. Many teachers have told me that seeing the EIR routines being applied in the classroom makes it easy to start teaching the EIR lessons. See this icon throughout the book for easy access to the video clips and teaching resources on the DVD.

Guidance for Monthly Sessions with Colleagues

In the last chapter, "Creating an EIR Community," I share a model for a professional learning community (PLC) that works. Over my many years of working with teachers on effective reading instruction generally, and EIR lessons specifically, I have learned from teachers' comments that the collaborative nature of learning new instructional techniques with colleagues leads to excellent understanding, reflection, and success.

Website Support

For additional support, go to www.Heinemann.com and search by Taylor or *Catching Readers* for answers to questions that will likely arise about teaching EIR lessons. Also, see the Heinemann website to learn more about the availability of additional support from an EIR expert.

We can help so many children become successful readers when we offer excellent reading instruction and provide effective interventions to those students who require additional reading support within their classroom setting. I am excited to have the opportunity to offer my *Catching Readers* series of books to you. Thank you for the important work you do for our children!

catching
readers

Helping Third Graders Who Struggle

· ·

Lessons That Sit Within Effective Reading Instruction

In third grade, children are no longer considered little kids, but they still have that unbridled enthusiasm for learning that makes teaching this grade so rewarding. They are old enough to be self-reliant and collaborative if they are given the opportunities. Most third graders read fairly fluently and have shifted from students who are learning to read to students who are reading to learn and to enjoy from a wide range of texts, including chapter books, nonfiction texts, and even material on the Internet. However, the range of students' reading abilities is wide. In the fall, most students read grade-level material fluently, some still read haltingly, and a number of them are reading well below grade level.

Catching Readers, Grade 3 is designed to help you meet the needs of your students who are in this considerable range of reading levels. Although the book's focus is primarily on assisting children who struggle to catch up or keep up with grade-level expectations for reading, you'll also learn about effective, differentiated reading instruction for all students.

My career as a researcher and teacher educator has been dedicated to studying and describing components of effective literacy instruction so that teachers can become more intentional in their teaching and more confident in their interactions with children around all aspects of reading instruction, including whole-class and small-group reading lessons, word recognition, vocabulary, and comprehension instruction, and more. And so this intervention model—Early Intervention in Reading (EIR®)—doesn't stand separate from but sits within the regular classroom literacy instruction. To illustrate how this model works, I highlight the work of three outstanding third-grade teachers who use EIR within their literacy block in Chapter 2. They find their students' reading abilities grow tremendously during the year. These teachers share their ideas about differentiated instruction to meet individual needs and the operation of an effective literacy block, during which children engage in lots of authentic reading, writing, and talk.

How the Early Intervention in Reading Model Sits Within Effective Reading Instruction

The small-group intervention lessons featured in this book are based on EIR, which is a set of teaching practices I developed that incorporates the characteristics of effective reading instruction (see page 3). The third-grade program has been in practice for more than fifteen years in schools, and if you're a teacher looking to implement response to intervention (RTI) or differentiated instruction, you'll see that my model can easily be viewed—and used—to meet these current calls to action. Early Intervention in Reading provides:

▶ third-grade students who are reading below grade level with an additional daily opportunity to interact with text in a structured, consistent, and comfortable small-group setting

▶ third-grade teachers with a framework that will show them how to support their students so they can catch up or keep up with grade-level expectations for reading

▶ teachers and schools an intervention model that isn't stigmatizing for children because it uses authentic literature and practices, and takes place within the regular classroom— and usually by the classroom teacher.

I want to emphasize that I developed this model with classroom teachers in mind—based on my belief that students shouldn't be pulled out of the classroom for extra help. Rather, teachers need to learn to support them during the daily reading block. They also need to harness the collective power of colleagues and work together to help all children learn to read well. Supplemental instruction for those who are struggling can't be something that only the special teachers of reading know about.

How EIR Meets the Requirements of Effective Reading Instruction

	Effective Reading Instruction	EIR Lessons
What You Teach (Content)	Word-recognition instruction	Decoding multisyllabic words, coaching in word-recognition strategies
	Rereading for fluency	Repeated reading of stories, coached reading with feedback
	Text-based vocabulary instruction	Discussion of word meanings at point of contact in EIR stories
	Comprehension strategies instruction	Summarizing stories, practicing comprehension monitoring, generating questions, answering written questions successfully
	Comprehension instruction in the context of high-level talk about text	Coaching for comprehension and high-level talk about text
How You Teach (Pedagogy)	Application of taught skills and strategies to text	Much of the EIR lesson involves applying taught skills and strategies to text
	Differentiated instruction	EIR lessons are an extra shot of quality instruction for struggling readers in which the teacher provides support to individual students based on need
	Balance direct teaching with providing support	After teaching skills and strategies, the teacher spends much of the EIR lesson coaching students to use these skills and strategies as they read EIR stories
	Teaching with clear purpose and good timing	Teacher states lesson purposes routinely, teaches daily steps of each 20-minute EIR lesson at a rapid pace
	Active student engagement	All students read, write, talk, and share in the small group or with a partner
	Student engagement in challenging, motivating learning activities	Students read engaging narrative and informational texts that they will then read and discuss with grade 1 reading buddies who are also in EIR groups. Third-grade students coach their younger reading buddies with their EIR stories as well.
	Developing independent learners	High expectations, releasing to students, partner work, developing students' self-confidence through their tutoring of younger readers who are experiencing difficulties in learning to read
	Motivating classroom community	Using praise, helpful feedback, demonstrating enthusiasm for learning
Professional Learning	Collaborative learning with a focus on practice	Monthly learning meetings to discuss EIR strategies, successes, and challenges

Through structured, 20-minute lessons, a group of struggling readers are provided with an extra shot of daily quality reading instruction. Teachers support and coach individual students based on need, so it accelerates students' reading progress. We'll look at the five-day lesson cycle in detail in Chapter 3, but here is a glimpse of how these lessons amplify the effective reading instruction.

Which Children Need the Intervention and What Is the End Goal?

Students who benefit from this intervention are those who enter third grade reading on an end-of-grade 1 or grade 2 reading level. The lessons focus on building students' reading fluency and comprehension. Ideally, the model uses a cross-age tutoring component in which students work for three days on a narrative or informational book that they will read on the fourth day to a first-grade student who is also reading below grade level (or to a grade 3 EIR partner).

Children who fall below 90 percent accuracy on a second-grade passage typically need supplemental help in word recognition. Children who read less than 65 words correctly per minute (wcpm) early in the fall on second- or third-grade-level texts most likely need to work on fluency. Children who can tell little about a second- or third-grade informal reading inventory passage (e.g., get a score of 1 or 2 on the summarizing rubric discussed in Chapter 5) or are at the frustration level (lower than 70 percent correct) on informal reading inventory questions may need to work on comprehension. In Chapter 5, I describe assessments you can use to determine which students might benefit from EIR.

Our goal is for the students to catch up with grade-level peers—and they do! Looking at data from almost 500 third-grade students reading a year or more below grade level in twenty schools, I found that 94 percent of the third graders receiving EIR lessons were able to decode third-grade level passages with at least 93 percent accuracy in word recognition on an informal reading inventory in May (Taylor 2001). Although work on fluency was still warranted, their mean fluency score went from 64 to 92 wcpm from the beginning to the end of the school year.

Teachers report that the children in the grade 3 EIR program take their tutoring very seriously and enjoy it immensely. In addition to improving students' reading ability, I have found that the cross-age tutoring component of the EIR program enhances students' attitudes and self-concepts as readers (Taylor et al. 1997).

The What and How of Good Third-Grade Teaching

EIR was developed with key elements of content (the what) and pedagogy (the how) as its foundation. Effective teachers tend to have a great day-to-day awareness of both content and pedagogy. With that in mind, in Chapter 2 you will meet three teachers, Karen Olson, Julie McCloskey, and Lauren Schwartz, and you will see what effective teaching looks like in urban, suburban, and rural settings. You'll gain a sense of how these teachers connect EIR lessons to their overall reading instruction. These three teachers not only teach EIR lessons, but also provide effective reading instruction to all their students and see excellent growth in their students' reading abilities during each school year.

Content: Four Dimensions Elementary Children Need

The content of effective reading instruction has many dimensions, all of which develop students' abilities to become competent readers. These dimensions, listed here, have a sound body of reading research behind them, as will be noted in the sections that follow:

- word-recognition development

- fluency development

- vocabulary development

- comprehension development

Does this list comprise a complete universe of what leads children to become successful, engaged readers? No, but these dimensions are the nonnegotiable aspects of teaching reading in third grade. Without them, all the other practices don't have a sufficient foundation.

Word-Recognition Development

Most students in kindergarten and first grade—and many in second grade—benefit from systematic, explicit instruction in phonemic awareness and phonics knowledge (Adams 1990; National Reading Panel [NRP] 2000; Snow, Burns, and Griffin 1998). Typically, by third grade most students, even those who are reading below grade level, know their symbol sound correspondences. However, many third-graders who are not yet reading on a third-grade level, benefit from phonics instruction that focuses on how to decode multisyllabic words. Coaching students to use word-recognition strategies as they read stories and informational texts is another important aspect of decoding instruction for below-grade-level readers. For example, when students in Lauren Schwartz's EIR group get stuck on the word *constitution* (one student has not looked carefully through the entire word and calls it *construction*), Lauren coaches students to break the word into chunks. They come up with *con-sti-tu-tion*. They have to be flexible with the /i/ sound in *sti*, trying the short *i* sound after first trying the long *i* sound, but do come up with the correct word and go on do discuss its meaning.

Fluency Development

Developing *fluency*, or reading at a good rate with appropriate phrasing, is important since fluent reading supports comprehension. Oral reading procedures to develop fluency, in which students receive guidance or support, can have a significant impact on the reading abilities of below-grade-level third-grade readers

(Kuhn and Stahl 2003). Procedures to build fluency include repeated reading and coached reading, as well as ample opportunities for students to read books at their independent and instructional reading levels. Effective reading instruction weaves fluency practice into whole-group and small-group lessons, as well as through independent work activities.

Vocabulary Development

When it comes to developing students' vocabulary, using a variety of approaches is critical. The approaches (Baumann and Kame'enui 2004; Blachowicz and Fisher 2000; Graves 2007) include:

 ▶ direct instruction in specific words

 ▶ prereading instruction in words

 ▶ learning to use strategies to determine word meanings

 ▶ learning of words in rich contexts and incidentally through wide reading

 ▶ studying words that children will find useful in many contexts (Beck et al. 2002)

Three points are worth emphasizing: First, some words need to be introduced *before* reading so that students are not confused about major aspects of a story. Second, teachers sometimes do insufficient vocabulary instruction *during* and *after* the reading of a story. Beck and colleagues (2002) stress the value of teaching many word meanings at point of contact in the text. When Julie McCloskey has students read in groups of three about animal behavior, she instructs them to look for "million dollar words" that describe the behaviors of the animals they are reading about. Later in a whole-group meeting, students will share their words and what they mean. Third, developing students' curiosity about words is also important. You can model this interest in word meanings and enthusiasm for authors' word choice in a variety of ways, and it's a boon to students' reading and writing. For example, Julie McCloskey talks with great energy about the words that describe animal behavior that students will find and share.

Comprehension Development

Skilled readers use strategies as they read to enhance their comprehension. Also, research has shown that explicit instruction in comprehension strategies improves students' reading comprehension abilities (Pressley 2006; Guthrie et al. 2000; NRP 2000). Explicit lessons are most effective in the following strategies: summarizing; comprehension monitoring; using graphic and semantic organizers before, during, and after reading; using story structure; answering questions; and generating questions (NRP 2000). Also, using multiple instructional strategies, like reciprocal teaching, in naturalistic contexts is important to students' growth in reading comprehension abilities (Guthrie et al. 2004;

Klingner et al. 2004; NRP 2000; Pressley 2006). The classroom examples in Chapter 2 of Karen, Julie, and Lauren exemplify instruction in comprehension strategies, including summarizing a story, summarizing informational text, asking and answering questions, clarifying, and using multiple comprehension strategies.

Teaching students how to engage in high-level talk and writing about text is another vital aspect of comprehension instruction repeatedly found to be related to reading gains (Knapp 1995; McKeown, Beck, and Blake 2009; Saunders and Goldenberg 1999; Taylor et al. 2003; Van den Branden 2000). For example, in Chapter 2, we read about Lauren Schwartz and her students discussing the character traits and actions of Miss Rumphius (in the book by the same name, Cooney [1982]) and see how this discussion leads them to one of the themes of the story: making the world a better place.

So, with these content elements under our belt, let's turn to the *how* behind the what: the essential pedagogy behind EIR lessons and all effective teaching.

Pedagogy: The Art of Teaching Demystified

You know good teaching when you see it, and yet, it can be hard to capture all the nuances of it in the confines of a book. In short, good teaching consists of all the teacher's routines and practices, as well as his or her ability to respond in the moment to students' needs and to connect to students so they feel motivated to learn. For example, techniques like clearly stating lesson purposes or offering impromptu coaching, as well as decisions that need to be made about things such as timing (e.g., how long to spend on a particular aspect of a lesson) or what texts and tasks to use to engage students in purposeful learning activities are part of the pedagogy of teaching.

Affective Dimensions: What It Means to Be Motivating to Kids

Another important aspect of pedagogy includes the "people skills" involved in teaching. Research and our own experiences have a lot to tell us about the impact of teachers' management, expectations, and attitudes toward learning on children's achievement and motivation. As you read the characteristics in the boxes that follow, think about your third-grade students and how you view yourself on these aspects of effective teaching.

Elements of Effective Pedagogy

Effective teachers skillfully coordinate many pedagogical aspects of their reading lessons. They make sure that they:

▶ Strike a good balance between whole-group and small-group instruction, using one form or another that best meets lesson objectives (Chorzempa and Graham 2006)

▶ Consider the purposes and timing of their lessons relative to their students' varying instructional needs

▶ Balance direct teaching (telling, leading) with differentiated support (e.g., coaching, providing feedback) as students are engaged in learning activities (Connor et al. 2004; Pressley et al. 2003; Taylor et al. 2003)

▶ Foster students' active involvement in literacy activities to enhance their learning and motivation (Guthrie et al. 2000)

▶ Provide students with challenging, motivating activities as they are working with the teacher, on their own, or with other students (Pressley et al. 2003)

▶ Sustain a balanced approach to instruction that involves direct teaching of reading skills and strategies as well as giving students opportunities to apply skills and strategies to engaging texts through reading, writing, and discussing (Pressley 2006)

▶ Provide differentiated instruction and make good choices in the use of instructional materials based on students' abilities and interests (Pressley et al. 2007)

▶ Sustain culturally responsive instruction, which includes teachers building on students' cultural strengths as they structure student interactions and use multicultural literature to celebrate students' cultural heritages and introduce students to new cultural perspectives (Au 2006)

▶ Continually assess students' engagement, understanding, and behavior throughout the day (Pressley et al. 2003)

▶ Systematically collect and share a variety of formal and informal student assessment data to help them make instructional decisions to improve student performance (Lipson et al. 2004; Taylor et al. 2000). Data might include diagnostic, formative (on-the-go assessment as kids work), and summative assessments (checking to see if students understand something at the end of learning).

Additional Motivating Pedagogical Practices

Effective teachers in the elementary grades:

▶ Maintain positive classroom atmospheres and teach with enthusiasm for learning (Dolezal et al. 2003; Pressley et al. 2003)

▶ Expertly manage and organize their classrooms (Dolezal et al. 2003; Pressley 2001, 2006; Taylor, Pressley, and Pearson 2002)

▶ Provide encouragement and praise as well as positive feedback (Pressley et al. 2007)

▶ Have high expectations for their students, communicate to students that effort leads to success, encourage independence and responsibility, provide students with choice, and foster cooperative learning experiences (Bohn et al. 2004; Dolezal et al. 2003; Guthrie et al. 2004; Hamre and Pianta 2005; Pressley et al. 2003)

Collaborate with Colleagues

▶ While individual teachers can positively improve upon their reading instruction and thus the development of their students' reading, it is often helpful to work with colleagues as you embark on the journey of being the most effective teacher you can be. Karen, Julie, and Lauren all believe that this collaboration piece is extremely instrumental to their success. They share some of their ideas on the value of collaboration in Chapter 2. In Chapter 7, I provide guidance on implementing EIR schoolwide.

Having a good grasp of the content and pedagogy of effective reading instruction will inform your practice and support you in the many decisions you make in your day-to-day reading lessons. In turn, effective practices will help your students develop into motivated, competent readers.

A Five-Day Cycle of Supplemental Instruction

Now that we have looked at effective reading instruction for all students, let's turn to an overview of the EIR model for students who need additional support. It is important that children who are not reading on grade level experience success in reading, and EIR is structured so this happens. The EIR model works on a five-day cycle. Its predictable structure provides consistency for struggling readers and helps build their confidence. During the five-day cycle of lessons, students are supported through the following practices:

▶ Active engagement

▶ Systematic word-recognition instruction

▶ Coaching in word-recognition strategies

▶ Repeated reading for fluency

▶ Comprehension and vocabulary instruction

▶ Guidance and support on their teaching and coaching of at-risk first-grade readers

▶ Regular monitoring of progress

Active Engagement

Students are busy participating in reading experiences throughout the 20-minute, small-group session. Within this time period, students engage in multiple activities that address different elements essential to learning to read. This 20-minute session is considered to be acceleration, unlike remediation, and implies that the children receiving this intervention can learn to read before they fall behind. In EIR, children typically enjoy the small-group routine and stay actively engaged during the lesson.

Repeated Reading for Fluency

Students read and reread texts. They read stories by taking turns, with a partner, and independently, which helps them experience fluent reading as well as the feeling of success. As they reread, their word-recognition accuracy, automaticity, and fluency develop.

Decoding Multisyllabic Words and Coaching in the Use of Multiple Word-Recognition Strategies

Decoding support is given while children read and involves modeling, asking questions, or giving prompts related to words children don't know. This coaching enables children to succeed at figuring out a word they don't instantly recognize while they are reading. Typically, in third grade, children need strategies and coaching support as they gain confidence in decoding multisyllabic words.

The coaching also helps children learn to self-monitor their word-recognition attempts. For example, if a child comes to a word, reads it incorrectly, and then self-corrects it, this is a good example of self-monitoring. Complementing children for their attempts (e.g., "Good checking, how did you know to try that word again?") is an integral part of the instruction, because the praise and questions encourage children to be aware of the strategies they are using to make sense of texts. You also want students to notice instances when words they say don't make sense in the context of the story or don't look like the actual word they are trying to read. Part of self-monitoring is learning to cross-check; that is, not only being sure a word looks like the word on the page, but also being sure that a word makes sense in the story, or vice versa.

Coaching to Develop Student Independence

An important part of coaching students in word-recognition strategies is releasing responsibility to the children as soon as possible. Typically, at first, you will have to model or demonstrate for them how to use a variety of strategies to figure out words they do not decode correctly and follow up this modeling with coaching as students try to sound out words themselves. Often, however, teachers inadvertently coach struggling readers too much for too long, and the students don't learn to depend on themselves as readers. As the year progresses, teachers need to use more general prompts (e.g., "What can you do?" Or, "Look at that again.") and focus on their wait time so that students have enough time to problem-solve and figure out words themselves. When I am coaching children, I feel successful when they come to a hard word in the text and don't look up at me for the answer. It's important to praise them for this independence and remind them that this is what they need to continue to do when they are reading on their own.

Comprehension Instruction and Vocabulary Development

Teaching struggling readers to read for meaning is very important, but it is sometimes neglected because the focus is on teaching students to develop their word-recognition fluency and ability to decode grade-level texts. To send the message that reading for meaning is what reading is all about, teachers in EIR lessons discuss the meanings of potentially unfamiliar words they come across in the story and ask questions about the text that:

▶ Expand students' comprehension of the story

▶ Stretch their thinking

▶ Relate the story or nonfiction passage to their lives

▶ Involve them in summarizing

As students answer thought-provoking questions, the teacher coaches them to elaborate on their ideas. I call this part of the EIR lesson "coaching for comprehension."

Regular Monitoring of Progress

Regular assessment of students' progress is important to their success in the EIR program and is a hallmark of effective teachers and schools (Lipson et al. 2004; Pressley et al., 2003; Taylor et al. 2000). Teachers need to monitor students' reading abilities frequently to know when to fine-tune their instruction. They may need to provide more help or they may need to release more responsibility to the students to accelerate their reading growth. The teacher conducts an oral reading analysis to assess students' progress in word-recognition accuracy, word attack strategies, and fluency. (See Chapter 4 for this assessment.) The teacher also assesses students' abilities to summarize and write answers to questions on texts. (See Chapter 5.)

How the EIR Model Sits Within a Balanced Literacy Block

Now, let's take a look at how you might fit EIR lessons into your day by organizing your instruction around 100- to 120-minute reading blocks.

Reading Block: A Sample Schedule

Karen Olson has a 110-minute reading block. She spends about 30 minutes a day on a whole-group lesson. She spends about 60 minutes a day on three guided reading groups and 20 minutes on one EIR group (a second shot of quality instruction for her struggling readers). Her schedule appears on page 13.

In the next chapter, you'll see how three teachers make the content and pedagogy of effective reading instruction—and the principles of EIR—come alive in their whole-group and small-group lessons. This taste of their teaching will help you set the intervention lessons within a context. In Chapter 6 we'll also return to our three teachers' classrooms to see how they organize their day to provide EIR lessons to students who need more support and offer motivating independent activities to all their students.

DISCUSS WITH YOUR COLLEAGUES

1. Discuss aspects of effective reading instruction (content and pedagogy) you feel are embedded in your teaching. What aspects do you think are thriving? What do you feel less sure of? How might you improve your reading instruction?

2. What's the one thing that concerns you the most in regard to your teaching? Were there some things in this chapter that gave you insights into solutions to this problem?

Reading Block: Karen's Sample Schedule

9:00–9:30 Whole-Group Lesson

▶ Use a selection from basal reader or a trade book

▶ Target a comprehension strategy

▶ Teach vocabulary at point of contact in the selection

▶ Pose and discuss answers to high-level questions

▶ Review learning activities for independent work time

9:30–10:50 Independent and Small-Group Work

Independent Work: While the teacher is working with small groups of students, the other students are working independently or with a partner or small group on challenging and differentiated materials (see Chapter 6 for a more in-depth discussion of independent work activities). For example, students might:

▶ Read new texts as directed by the teacher

▶ Write in a journal or on open-ended response sheets about what they have read

▶ Talk with others about what they have read

▶ Write down new or interesting vocabulary and possible word meanings

▶ Read/reread books in their book baskets or book bags

Small-Group 1 (9:30–9:50)

Using a story in a text at students' reading level, the teacher

▶ Provides instruction in decoding multisyllabic words, as needed

▶ Coaches students in word-recognition strategies as they read their leveled text

▶ Discusses a few word meanings prior to reading, but focuses more on vocabulary at point of contact in the story and after reading

▶ Follows up on the comprehension strategy targeted in whole-group lesson

▶ Poses and discusses answers to high-level questions on leveled text

Small-Group 2 (9:50–10:10)

Follow same strategies as small-group 1.

Small-Group 3 (10:10–10:30)

Follow same strategies as small-group 1.

EIR Lesson (10:30–10:50)

▶ Follow EIR strategies. (Note that these students were also in one of the small groups.)

Meet the Teachers

• •

The Differentiated Lessons and Teacher Collaboration That Support EIR

Karen Olsen, Julie McCloskey, and Lauren Schwartz, the teachers high-lighted in this chapter, are connected to my work on effective instruc-tion and the EIR framework. Vignettes from their reading lessons are shared so that you can see how the teachers support and echo the reading con-tent and pedagogy of reading and EIR lessons. You'll read the teachers' own words as they share the benefits of engaging in professional development with colleagues. Struggling third graders will excel farther if you take on EIR as a group, whether you team up with teachers at your grade level, in the primary grades, or as a schoolwide initiative.

The three teachers in this chapter teach in different schools with different student populations and needs. Table 2-1 highlights this diversity.

Diversity in the Highlighted Teachers' Schools

Teacher	Years Teaching	School Setting	Percent of Students Who Receive Subsidized Lunch	Percent English Language Learners
Karen	5	Rural	65	6
Julie	10	Suburban	40	12
Lauren	20	Urban	70	25

Table 2-1 Diversity in the Highlighted Teachers' Schools

The Teachers

Karen teaches third grade at Lakeside Elementary, a school in a small, rural town where 65 percent of the students receive subsidized lunch and 6 percent are ELL students, primarily native Spanish speakers. Karen has been teaching for five years, and she learned how to teach EIR lessons in the second year of her school's reading improvement project. Karen's students grew by a mean of 7 normal curve equivalent points (NCEs) during the third year of the school-based reform effort, ending the year with a mean NCE comprehension score of 57 (which corresponds to the 63rd percentile).

Julie teaches third grade at Brookstone Elementary, a suburban school where 40 percent of the students receive subsidized lunch and 12 percent are ELL students, primarily Hmong, Somali, and Spanish speakers. Julie has been teaching for 10 years, and was new to Brookstone in the second year of the school reform in reading project. She learned how to teach EIR intervention lessons in her first year at Brookstone. Her students grew by a mean of 8 NCEs during their second-grade year, ending the year with a mean NCE comprehension score of 53 (50th percentile, up from the 45th NCE, or 40th percentile, in the fall).

Lauren teaches third grade at Roosevelt Elementary School where 75 percent of the students receive subsidized lunch and 25 percent speak English as a second language. Lauren has been teaching for 20 years, participated in study groups as part of a schoolwide reading improvement project for three years, and learned how to deliver EIR intervention instruction through participation in an EIR study group in the second year of her the school's reading improvement process. In the third year of the school change project, Lauren's students grew by an average of nine NCEs on the Gates MacGinitie Reading test from fall to spring, ending the school year with a mean comprehension score at the 55th NCE, or 60th percentile.

Common Factors in Students' Success

While these teachers have different styles and work in different settings, there are similarities in practices and recent changes to their instruction that are instrumental to the success of their teaching and the reading achievement of their students.

When asked what components were critical to the success of her classroom reading program and the changes to her instruction that made it more effective, Karen mentioned she is more confident about:

▶ Motivating students and engaging them

▶ Providing reading material at the child's appropriate level

▶ Differentiating instruction with the help of ongoing assessments and the EIR lessons

She also thinks her reading instruction has improved especially in these three aspects:

▶ Asking more high-level questions

▶ Teaching strategies instead of skills and using reciprocal teaching more

▶ Doing less talking and having the kids talk more

For Julie, the success of her reading program is attributed to:

▶ Purposeful planning and knowing her reasons for what she is teaching and identifying the end result

▶ Differentiating her teaching based on where her students are with their reading and what they need to improve

▶ Having high expectations and keeping her focus on accelerating students beyond their starting point with reading

Julie highlights the following components and routines as instrumental:

▶ Focusing on summaries and teaching vocabulary in context

▶ Using book clubs and letting students have conversations

▶ Teaching EIR lessons

▶ Working on more participation by her students and less by her

▶ Giving students choices

Lauren thinks that the EIR model and professional development in reading helped her realize that struggling readers can not excel if the overall program isn't sufficiently focused on differentiation. Identifying the third graders who would benefit from tailored instruction forces a practitioner to take on full-scale differentiated, effective reading instruction. Teachers must meet all students' needs and attend to everyone's engagement and growth. Lauren mentions as crucial:

▶ Having a classroom environment that is completely conducive to learning

▶ Differentiating instruction and reteaching as needed at students' level

▶ Planning for and using research-based practices and strategies

▶ Focusing on comprehension

▶ Getting everyone involved in the lessons

▶ Teaching strategies more directly

▶ Expecting her students to think a lot more than they used to

Teacher Talk

I share the teacher quotes that follow to cheerlead you as you embark on learning to teach EIR lessons as one aspect of your classroom reading program. Whether you are a beginning or veteran teacher, the implementation of EIR will help your struggling readers make good growth in reading during their third-grade year. Here's what Karen, Julie, and Lauren had to say when I asked them how professional learning, including EIR, changed their instruction.

The Influence of Collaborative Professional Learning on Teaching Practice

KAREN: I am constantly reflecting, modifying, and fine-tuning my instructional practices. I think that study groups, particularly cross-grade groups, have contributed the most to my development. We have developed a common language. We share ideas and support each other.

JULIE: Without professional development based on research and the desire to change along with the students, you aren't going to grow. We constantly are reflecting by sharing the videos of our teaching and thinking about ways to change to help our students be successful.

LAUREN: I think the study groups where you really reflect on your teaching and get peer input gets you to notice aspects of students' learning that you might have missed. For example, we are just starting to realize how important it is to get kids to synthesize, evaluate, and do enrichment projects that motivate them. Learning to teach EIR lessons has been good, too, since it helps so many students who are a little behind the rest in reading.

Biggest Benefits to Student Learning

When asked about the biggest benefits to student learning, again the teachers have similar responses.

KAREN: The quality of my students' journal writing, the skill they demonstrate in book club discussions, the inferences they draw from what they read—none of these would have occurred if I hadn't had the opportunity to change my *instructional practices. The students have become deeper thinkers. They are making more connections with their reading. They are becoming quite comfortable with the four elements of reciprocal teaching. We see on the MCA [state] test that this has transferred to student achievement.*

JULIE: *My students have more knowledge of strategies than before, and they are more confident in their reading abilities. Also, they have an eagerness to read and to learn. They are excited about picking up a book, and they really like informational text.*

LAUREN: *I see kids interacting with text more and I see them making text-to-text connections by comparing stories and characters, and relating the text to themselves. Also, I am thrilled that they are going back to the text to support their ideas. When you ask them about the author's message, they are understanding this and it shows when they write their own stories. I think I've learned how to coach kids by being coached myself. This year I'm not the leader in book clubs anymore; the kids are really in charge. They won't even look at me now; they just look at the leader, which is great.*

On the following pages, detailed descriptions of these three teachers' reading lessons provide examples of what effective reading instruction looks like in practice. You will see how different teachers incorporate elements of effective reading instruction into their teaching based on their own styles and, of course, their students' needs. Notice how the teachers integrate the various components of content including instruction in word recognition, fluency, vocabulary, and comprehension, as well as elements of pedagogy including direct teaching and coaching; differentiation; and intellectually challenging independent, partner, and small-group activities.

Sample Lesson: Karen
Understanding Story Characters

Karen wants her students to become independent readers and thinkers who are responsible for their learning. As we can see in her lesson, her students have made some giant strides toward these goals. They work well in small groups, they are developing strong discussion skills, and they are able to back up their ideas and opinions by citing evidence from the texts they are reading.

Large-Group Lesson

Karen begins her whole-group lesson by teaching students how to complete a character map to better understand a story. She tells them, "A character map helps you better understand a character in any book you read. Paying close attention to a character often helps you understand one or more themes of the story. Today we are going to start on a character map of Molly from our story, *Molly's Pilgrim* (Cohen 2005). We will look for clues about Molly's background, appearance, problems, actions, and personality, as well as changes in Molly over the course of the story."

Karen begins reading and then stops to ask, "What do we know about Molly?" Students offer, "She is Russian. She is probably not a real Pilgrim." Karen coaches for elaboration, "Why do you say that?" The student responds, "She came in the 1880s." Karen explains, "She is an immigrant, a person who moved from one country to another." Karen prompts for more information about Molly. Students reply, "She is different than her classmates. She speaks a different language. Some kids tease her." They fill out parts of their character map with their learning partner. Karen explains, "As you read, I want you to jot down more ideas you have about Molly's character on the character map. Discuss your ideas with your learning partner. We'll share these when we meet tomorrow in whole group."

Small Guided Reading Groups

For small-group lessons, Karen has students working on three books, based on their reading level, that tie in with their social studies work on the Colonial and Revolutionary War periods in American history. On this particular day she spends about 10 minutes with the first group and 15 to 20 minutes with each of the other two groups. In each group, students are working on a character map of the main character in their book. The first small group is a book club where they are, for the most part, involved in a discussion on their own. Karen guides the second and third groups, but she is teaching them to become more independent in discussions of what they read. Students in groups 2 and 3 are reading their guided reading books and answering questions that Karen has written on the board until she calls them to her reading table.

First, Karen checks with a group of advanced readers who are working independently as a book club on *Sign of the Beaver* (Speare 1984). In this group, each member is assigned a reciprocal teaching role (Palincsar and Brown 1984, 1986): *predictor*, *questioner*, *summarizer*, and *clarifier*. These roles change during the course of the discussion. Students create open-ended response sheets with questions they have generated. The questioner reads a question and students write their own answers and then discuss them. If there is a disagreement as they discuss the book, the clarifier has them read from their book to help them work through their discussion. The clarifier also has them check the book for context clues when they have trouble with a word's meaning. Karen reminds students to save time to work on their character map of Matt, the main character in the book, before she moves on to another group.

Karen moves to group of less skilled readers who are reading *Sam the Minuteman* (Benchley 1987). She listens to students reread brief sections of the story one at a time and she coaches them in word-recognition strategies if they get stuck. Then, they work on a character map for the character Sam Brown. Karen comments, "I would like you to share one thing about Sam. We are each going to listen to the person sharing. Let's not raise hands. Wait until someone is done for your turn to talk." Then, students work on their character maps and continue to write answers to questions as Karen moves on to the third group.

This group consists of students who are average readers. They are reading *A Lion to Guard Us* (Bulla 1989). Karen begins, "Let's have a conversation, starting with the first question, *In what ways did Amanda's life change when her mother died?* We have practiced talking in a conversational way before, not raising hands. Let's practice that again today as we talk about Amanda and her character traits." Karen has the students look in the book to find evidence to support their ideas. She reminds them to work on a character map of Amanda after they are done with their discussion. Students continue their discussion and then have a vote to determine how many chapters to read next.

 To help you get more ideas about the complex task of integrating the many aspects of effective reading instruction into your teaching, review a second sample lesson by Karen on the DVD, Appendix 2-1. The lesson focuses on the comprehension strategies of predicting, clarifying, questioning, and summarizing informational text. Looking across Karen's two lessons, it is clear that she provides excellent, differentiated instruction as she teaches a comprehension strategy in whole group and reinforces this strategy in guided reading groups. Her instruction is intellectually challenging, students' independent activities are motivating and require high-level thinking, and students are actively engaged. These lessons also offer good examples of collaborative work and student choice.

Sample Lesson: Julie
Applying Reading Strategies to Informational Texts

Whole-Class Lesson

Julie enjoys teaching students how to read informational texts and believes this is very important since it is something they struggle with. Below, Julie provides an excellent example of collaborative learning activities with informational text and also gives good examples of differentiated instruction.

She begins her lesson with a review, "We have been talking about asking ourselves questions as we read to monitor our comprehension and to make sure we understand what the book is saying. Good readers stop and think and ask themselves questions. Why do we think and ask questions when we read?" Students answer, "To learn." "To know more about the world." "To understand new words."

Julie continues, "I suggested something to you when you read nonfiction. After you read a paragraph, you should ask yourself, *What did I just read?* This reminds you to summarize and then ask yourself, *Should I move on?* But what if you don't have a good understanding of what you read? Then what might you do?" A student answers, "Go back and read." Julie responds, "Yes, that's one good strategy. Maybe you got distracted. Why do readers summarize?" Another student replies, "To get a big picture in their head." Julie elaborates, "The most important points, you're summarizing as a way of reviewing them and making sure you've kind of gathered them all in your head as you read on." Julie then states the connection between the purpose of this lesson and the next, "Now, in small groups we will work on posters about the poisonous animals we are reading about. We will want to share the big picture, or in other words, summarize the most important ideas on our posters. Then groups will share what they have learned with other groups."

Small-Group Work

Students are working in small groups reading and writing about poisonous animals like snakes, dart frogs, and puffer fish. Julie differentiates instruction by meeting at the reading table with a few students who need more support. They bring their written work with them to the group. Julie asks students at the group to share what is on their posters. She coaches them so that they will be successful when they share with others. "What are you going to tell people about a puffer fish? How will you summarize? What is important for them to know?"

By having students count off for their animal groups, Julie divides the whole class into new small groups in which students share what they have learned about different poisonous animals. Julie asks, "Who can tell me the purpose of these posters?" A student answers, "To help people learn more about dangerous animals." Julie agrees, "Yes, when we read nonfiction, the purpose is to learn information. Please go to the right area of the room. Share with the rest of your new small group what you have learned and summarized about your animal. Those of you who are listening, you are to listen well and walk away with two new facts. Also, you can ask questions. At the end, I will call on you by pulling name sticks out of our name can to see what you learned. Your posters will be collected tomorrow."

Independent Activity

After the whole-group activity and before Julie begins to work with guided reading groups, she talks about an independent activity for students to work on with a partner during small-group time. She says, "We have books on the back table about our solar system. Pick one planet and write on this sheet about the size, miles from earth and the sun, number of moons, and interesting facts related to your planet. You will have to look at the table of contents and find the right places to look in your book for the information I want you to find about your planet." Julie also gives ideas for reading a difficult word such as working with a partner on decoding, skipping it, and breaking it into chunks. She closes by saying, "This is another way that we are using nonfiction books to find and summarize information. Any questions about what you are to do? We'll share our facts about the different planets tomorrow."

Sample Lesson: Lauren
Summarizing Narrative Text and Discussing the Author's Message

In the lesson that follows, Lauren provides a good example of differentiated instruction on summarizing a story. She regularly offers positive, enthusiastic feedback. Students are actively engaged by working with a partner, actively reading multiple books during the literacy block.

Whole-Group Lesson

Lauren begins by reviewing the strategy of summarizing narrative text, "What's a strategy you can use while you read?" Students say they can summarize. Lauren continues, "How do you do that?" One student answers, "Tell all the important ideas." Lauren coaches the student to tell her more. The student says, "You tell something about the beginning, middle, and end. And tell the author's message." Lauren elaborates, "Good readers do that every time they read because it helps them think." Lauren asks for more ideas, "What other strategy can we use?" Students say they can ask questions. Lauren asks for examples and students offer, "I wonder what he is going to do next? Which character am I more like?" Lauren coaches by asking students why good readers ask these kinds of questions. Students reply, "So you can get smarter." "To understand." "To know what you are reading." "To make it more interesting." Lauren prompts, "What's the difference between a big, fat juicy question and a skinny, dry question?" Students answer, "Fat juicy questions are longer; skinny questions you can answer by looking in the book; you have to think for the fat questions."

Lauren asks students to open their reading books to *Miss Rumphius* (Cooney 1982). She tells them, "Good readers summarize what is happening and they think about how they feel about the characters. They think about what the author is trying to say to them. Last week we read about Wilma Rudolph and summarized. What was the message in that biography?" Students say, "Don't give up." Lauren continues, "We will be summarizing *Miss Rumphius*. Read silently and then work with a partner to summarize in writing on our story summary sheet. Tell about the character and setting in the beginning, the problem and events in the middle, and the solution and author's message at the end. Also come up with a few big, fat questions. Then answer these together."

Small-Group Work Within a Whole-Class Lesson

Lauren differentiates instruction by calling five students who need more support back to a table to work with her while others work with partners. She reads aloud a few pages and students follow along silently. Next, Lauren and the small group of students read a few pages aloud together, and then students read the rest of the story on their own as Lauren coaches individual students. At the end, they discuss and summarize the beginning, middle, and end of the story together.

Return to Whole Group

After the small-group work, all students come back together to one group. Lauren asks, "We are trying to figure out the author's message. What happened at the end of the story? What is the author's message?" A student offers, "You should try to make the world a better place like Miss Rumphius did." A few students share their summaries and questions from their partner work. Pairs turn in their response sheets so Lauren can look over what they have done.

Follow-Up in Small-Group Lessons

In guided reading groups, Lauren reviews summarizing a story and generating important questions. She asks one group, "What is summarizing?" A student says, "Telling important details." Lauren coaches, "Not details." The student corrects his response, "Important parts." Lauren continues, "Good readers summarize to help them remember what is happening as they read. I do this with my long chapter books. You can do this with every book you read. How many of you summarize while you read?" Every hand goes up. "You need to be able to summarize what you are reading, otherwise you better read it again. Yesterday we were summarizing as we went along. Today, I'll have you summarize at the end of your story, just like we did in our whole-group lesson." Lauren goes over the directions for partners to read, summarize, and come up with big, fat, juicy questions on their response sheet. Before sending them off to work together, she tells them, "We'll go over our summaries and answer our questions tomorrow."

Follow-Up During Independent Work Time

Students have been assigned to book clubs by reading level. On this particular day, during independent work time, students are to read and generate good discussion questions in preparation for their book clubs that will meet the following day.

Support for Struggling Readers

On the DVD you can find a second lesson by Lauren that focuses on teaching an EIR lesson in a small group (see Appendix 2-2).

Schoolwide Dimensions of Effective Reading Instruction and EIR Interventions

Take a moment to think about your own school, and how you might collaborate with one or more of your colleagues to implement EIR within a shared vision of effective reading instruction.

The best teaching possible arises from schools in which teachers develop a shared set of understandings and beliefs about teaching and learning in general, and teaching reading in particular. Considerable research in the last decade has identified the following characteristics of schoolwide reading programs that support teachers' abilities to increase students' reading abilities. These schools have:

▶ a unified vision for teaching reading in every grade and a cohesive, schoolwide program (Taylor, Raphael, and Au, in press; Taylor et al. 2005)

▶ a substantial number of minutes and designated blocks of time devoted to reading instruction across different grades (Taylor et al. 2000)

▶ a schoolwide assessment plan in which student data are collected and used regularly to inform instruction (Pressley et al. 2003; Taylor et al. 2000; Taylor et al. 2002)

▶ interventions in place to meet the students' needs who are experiencing reading difficulties, who have special education needs, and who are English language learners (Foorman and Torgesen 2001; Mathes et al. 2005; Taylor et al. 2000)

▶ effective parent partnerships (Edwards 2004; Taylor, Pressley, and Pearson 2002)

An individual teacher working hard on her own to enhance her practice can make a huge difference in the lives of the students in her class. And yet, it is ideal to have an effective schoolwide reading program in place, whereby a common vision, time to work together, and a culture of peer support are part of your school's DNA. As Karen, Julie, and Lauren, and so many other teachers will attest, working with colleagues can provide amazing support. It's hard to examine and critique your own practice. Trusted colleagues can watch you teach, give you feedback, point out your strengths, and offer ideas to enhance your instruction in certain areas. This support helps you look closely at your practice, make modifications, and in the end, teach as effectively as possible so all of your students become skilled, motivated readers.

I hope that you carry this overview of effective reading instruction with you as you read about EIR strategies in the next chapter. Also, consider exploring the content, pedagogy, and interpersonal skills of exemplary teachers further. Professional books and research articles abound on many of the components of effective reading instruction discussed in Chapters 1 and 2. (Also see pages in the endmatter for Recommended Professional Readings.)

DISCUSS WITH YOUR COLLEAGUES

1. Discuss each of the three teachers described in this chapter. What do you like about their lessons? What questions do you have? As a group, is there one strand of effective reading instruction you would like to explore more?

2. Discuss instructional ideas you might try after reading about Karen, Julie, and Lauren.

The Five-Day Lesson Routine

• •

Now, it's time to look at the daily routine of the EIR lessons, the rationale behind them, and some basic getting started information. But first, let's review a few foundational ideas:

▶ With EIR, students' reading progress is accelerated because your instruction is based on the same effective reading instruction you use with *all* students—this is not about remediation.

▶ Students who are struggling with reading are given an extra shot of quality, small-group reading instruction. These children are getting this support in addition to, not instead of, other whole-group, small-group, and one-on-one attention.

▶ Engaging children's books are selected for the lessons (see the sample book list in Table 3-1 on page 32 and on the DVD to guide you).

▶ Third graders who need continued support in word-attack strategies for multisyllabic words are given the help they need. Additionally, many children who had a slow start in learning to read in first and second grade need to work on their reading fluency. Many also need to work on their reading comprehension. With the grade 3 EIR strategies, all of these things are covered. Although comprehension is not neglected, the focus for the first half of the year is on refining students' word-recognition strategies and their fluency. In the second half of the year, the focus shifts to improving reading comprehension while maintaining students' word-recognition accuracy and reading fluency.

Getting Started: FAQs

In Chapter 5 you will find more information about how to determine which children might benefit from EIR. For now, here are some questions teachers commonly ask about setting up the groups.

How many students are in a group?

Each group should have about five to seven students, seven being the maximum. If there are more than seven children in your room who need EIR lessons, I would recommend finding a way to have two groups instead of just one. If you have Title 1 at your school, perhaps the Title 1 teacher can work with one group and you can work with the other. Then you can periodically switch groups so you have a sense of the strengths and weaknesses of all your struggling readers.

Who should teach the EIR students?

As hard as it is to teach two EIR groups, should you find you need to do this, I cannot recommend that one of the groups be taught by an instructional aide. Children at risk of reading failure desperately need quality, supplemental reading instruction, which is in addition to instruction from the regular reading program, and which is provided by certified teachers.

What advice do you have in regard to English Language Learners and EIR?

Often the question comes up as how to handle English language learners (ELLs) and fall placement in EIR. I would put the ELLs in an EIR group in the fall unless they have the opportunity to learn to read in their first language. I have found that ELLs generally do well in EIR (Taylor 2001).

How do students in special education fare with EIR?

I have also found that EIR works well with students who have learning disabilities. No modifications to the program are recommended.

However, students who are developmentally and cognitively delayed learn well in EIR, but easier texts are typically needed than those used in regular EIR lessons to keep the children feeling successful.

Do the children in EIR groups feel stigmatized?

Over the many years I've been implementing and researching EIR, teachers report that children do not feel stigmatized. In fact, children love the fast pace, interesting texts, and feelings of success that they experience in EIR lessons. Children who no longer need the program often do not want to give the group up. All children are in small groups with their teacher, so no one seems to think much about who is with the teacher when. But the children in EIR lessons like the extra time with their teacher if she is the one teaching the EIR group.

What's the optimum time of the year to start EIR?

It is best to begin EIR in October. However, if you have just bought or been given this book and it is February, then for you, February would be the best time to begin. (It's just not a good idea to start any later in the year than March.)

What's the best way for me to begin to build my confidence with EIR?

After you read through the five-day procedures in Figure 3-1, read the Day 1 procedures again and watch the corresponding Day 1 video clips on the accompanying DVD. Soon, the EIR routines will seem very natural, and, as many teachers have reported, you will feel that the extra work on your part is worth the effort! For the past 15 years, I have consistently found that teachers, by February, are very excited about the progress they see their struggling third-grade readers making.

How do I know when I am ready to actually teach the lessons?

Once you have read this book, you may not feel completely ready to conduct the lessons, but I have found the best way to learn about EIR procedures is to just jump in and try them. If you have questions, and I'm sure you will, you can reread parts of the book or rewatch particular video clips. Ideally, you will be working with a group of colleagues learning and implementing EIR together so that you can share successes and discuss questions and uncertainties together.

Grade 3 Basic EIR Procedures

DAY 1 LESSON

1. The teacher and the students read a book they have not read before. The teacher models and assists in decoding multisyllabic words as students are reading. The teacher and students discuss word meanings in context.

2. The teacher coaches for comprehension on questions that engage students in high-level thinking.

3. Students practice reading their new book.

DAY 2 LESSON

1. The teacher coaches for comprehension.

2. The teacher and the students complete a group sheet on summarizing a narrative story (see Figure 3-5) or answer written questions on an informational book (see Figure 3-6 for examples).

3. The children practice rereading their book as the teacher coaches individuals in word recognition, providing help with multisyllabic words.

4. The teacher explains how to use the individual take-home sheet (see Figure 3-7), which prepares students for working with their first-grade partner (or EIR partner).

DAY 3 LESSON

1. The teacher gives students feedback on the take-home sheet. You should have students complete this sheet on Day 3 if it is not sent home.

2. Students practice reading the EIR first-grade book (if available) so they are sure they can successfully coach their first-grade partner.

3. The teacher and students discuss strategies for coaching first graders.

4. Students practice reading their grade 3 EIR book if they indicate on their take-home sheet that they need more practice. The teacher can conduct an oral reading analysis or an oral reading fluency check at this time.

However, if the cross-age tutoring piece is not in place, have EIR partners coach one another as they take turns reading their story and use their take-home sheets to discuss vocabulary and talk about the story.

DAY 4 LESSON

1. Third graders read their story to their first-grade partners.

2. Third graders work with first graders on comprehension and vocabulary from ideas on their individual take-home sheets.

3. Third graders listen as first graders read their EIR story and coach as needed.

DAY 5 LESSON

1. The teacher and students discuss the partner reading experience from the previous day. They talk about things that went well, share problems, and talk about solutions to problems.

2. There are several activities to choose from for Step 2. Using a text at their grade level, the teacher and students read a short selection and focus on attacking multisyllabic words, discuss vocabulary, summarize, and generate and answer thought-provoking comprehension questions. Or, students engage in independent reading as the teachers conducts an oral reading analysis or oral reading fluency check on one or more students. Or, the teacher assesses students' abilities to write summaries for short texts or to write answers to high-level thinking and comprehension strategy questions. Remember, you will spend two days on Day 5 activities (skipping Day 4 activities) if the cross-age tutoring component is not in place.

Figure 3-1 Grade 1 Basic EIR Procedures

Cross-Age Tutoring (or Partner Work)

Ideally, EIR instruction is done within the context of a cross-age tutoring program in which third-grade students tutor first-grade EIR students—or any first-grade students who need reading support. The third-grade children meet for 20 minutes a day for three days to prepare to work with younger EIR students on the fourth day. On the fourth day, they read a picture book or section of a longer book to their younger students and listen to the first graders read their own EIR story. On the fifth day, the third-grade students use the word-recognition, vocabulary, and comprehension strategies they have been practicing with their EIR books as they read from grade-level classroom textbooks. This work on Day 5 helps to build their confidence reading grade-level material.

Teachers report that the cross-age tutoring focus of the grade 3 EIR model appeals to their students and gives them a reason for working on their reading other than "to catch up because they are behind." Also, these students are proud to have been selected to work with younger students in reading and look forward to and enjoy working with their tutees. Research supports the efficacy of cross-age tutoring efforts as well (Guzetti 2002).

If you are unable to set up the cross-age tutoring component of EIR lessons, then on Day 3, students work with a partner in the EIR group instead. They reread their story to one another, discuss the questions they generated, and talk about the meanings of the vocabulary they identified on their take-home sheets. Day 5 activities are completed on both Day 4 and Day 5 if you are not able to do the cross-age tutoring.

A Word About Using EIR Books

The children all work on the same book for the week. Books are either narrative or informational books. The teacher selects relatively short books that will appeal to third and first graders and are written at a second- to third-grade reading level. (See Table 3-1 for a list of exemplar books for the grade 3 program.) More on selecting books for EIR lessons can be found at the end of this chapter.

As explained earlier, the comprehension activities for the narrative and informational books are somewhat different. Since narrative books tend to be easier, in the first half of the year, I recommend using more narrative than informational books as children work on fluency. During the second half of the year, I recommend using more informational than narrative books so children can work on their comprehension of informational text.

Grade 3 Exemplar Book Titles

Keep in mind that these books should be at a second- to third-grade reading level and appeal to first-grade reading partners.

Type of Book	Book Title	Author
Narrative Books	*George and Martha, Tons of Fun*	James Marshall
	Gila Monsters Meet You at the Airport	Marjorie Sharmat
	Martha Blah Blah	Susan Meddaugh
	Space Case	Edward Marshall
	When I Am Old with You	Angela Johnson
	Big Mama's	Donald Crews
Easy Readers (Narrative) (spend approximately two weeks per book by dividing the book into halves)	*Amelia Bedelia and the Surprise Shower*	Peggy Parish
	Clara and the Bookwagon	Nancy Levinson
	Come Back, Amelia Bedelia	Peggy Parish
	Mouse Tales	Arnold Lobel
	Wagon Wheels	Barbara Brennan
Informational Books (spend approximately two weeks per book by dividing the book into halves)	*It's a Fruit, It's a Vegetable, It's a Pumpkin* (Rookie Read-About Science Series)	Allan Fowler
	From Seed to Plant (Spend only 1 week on this book.)	Gail Gibbons
	Baby Whales Drink Milk (Let's-Read-and-Find-Out Science: Stage 1)	Barbara Ebensen
	Look Out for Turtles (Let's-Read-and-Find-Out Science: Stage 2)	Melvin Burger
	A Look at Teeth (Rookie Read About Science)	Allan Fowler
	Monster Bugs (Step-into-Reading, Step 3)	Lucille Penner
	Snakes Are Hunters	Patricia Lauber
	Amazing Buildings (DK Reader, Level 2)	Deborah Lock
	Desert Mammals (A True Book)	Elaine Landau
	Ocean Mammals (A True Book)	Elaine Landau

Table 3-1 *Grade 3 Exemplar Book Titles*

To recap, the weekly model shifts students to working with a first grader on Day 4 (or EIR partner on Day 3), which boosts their confidence as capable readers and mentors:

▶ Students have three days of 20-minute, small-group instruction with a relatively short narrative or informational book that is written on a second- to beginning-third-grade level. Instruction focuses on decoding multisyllabic words, fluency, vocabulary, comprehension strategies (summarizing, questioning), and high-level talk about text.

▶ Ideally, one day is devoted to reading the practiced book to a first-grade student and tutoring on their own EIR text.

▶ One day may focus on application of EIR strategies to classroom textbooks (or two days may focus on this if the cross-age tutoring is not in place).

1. The teacher and students read a book they have not read before. The teacher models and assists in decoding multisyllabic words as students are reading. He or she should discuss word meanings in context.

2. The teacher coaches for comprehension.

3. Students practice reading their new book.

Day 1, Step 1: Read Story and Work on Word Recognition and Vocabulary

(10 min.)

As you and your students begin reading the book chorally or by taking turns for the first part of the book, you provide on-the-spot teaching of word-recognition strategies as children come to words they don't know. It is important to continually remind other students to not call out a word if you are working with one child on decoding. You may not have time to read all the way through the book, but students can finish reading their book in Step 3.

Use a consistent strategy with the students for attacking multisyllabic words (Taylor et al. 1995; see Figure 3-2). Also, remind the children regularly that this is a strategy they can use when they are reading on their own. The strategy works best with words already in students' listening vocabulary, and many of the words struggling readers come across in their EIR texts will, in fact, be words in their listening vocabulary because the books are slightly below grade level.

Strategy for Decoding Multisyllabic Words

1. Break the word into chunks (approximate syllables) with one vowel (or vowel team) per chunk.

2. Be flexible as you sound out the chunks, especially with the vowel sounds. If one sound doesn't work, try another (refer to the Advanced Vowel Chart, Figure 3-3).

3. Remember to use context clues.

4. After you sound out the chunks, try it again only faster.

5. Remember that this will only get you close to the right word. Keep thinking of context.

Figure 3-2 Strategy for Decoding Multisyllabic Words

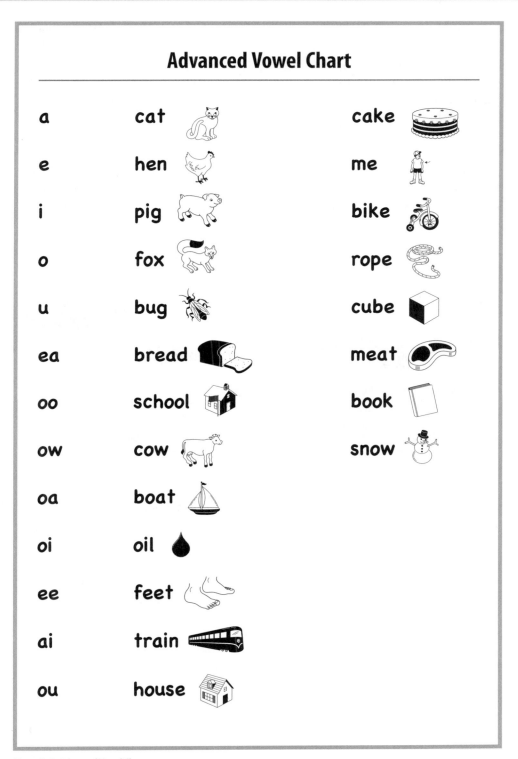

Advanced Vowel Chart

a	cat		cake	
e	hen		me	
i	pig		bike	
o	fox		rope	
u	bug		cube	
ea	bread		meat	
oo	school		book	
ow	cow		snow	
oa	boat			
oi	oil			
ee	feet			
ai	train			
ou	house			

Figure 3-3 Advanced Vowel Chart

It really doesn't matter if the children break a word into the exact syllables or not as found in the dictionary. Instead, they need to know that a chunk, or an approximate syllable, has one vowel or vowel team per chunk. They need to learn to be flexible with their sounding out of syllables and blending syllables together. They should be given a copy of the advanced vowel chart (see Figure 3-3) to help them remember the most common sounds for a particular vowel or vowel team. Consistently remind students that if one sound doesn't work, they should try another.

Also, remind the children frequently that their sounding out will only get them close to the real word. As they are blending syllables together, they need to think of a word that is close to what they are saying and that make sense in the story. I often find that children don't rely on context enough as an additional support when they are sounding out multisyllabic words.

see it iN ActioN

DAY 1
Decoding Long Words

Betsy Larson and her third-grade students begin to read the first story from *George and Martha, Tons of Fun* (Marshall 1986) that they will read to their first-grade reading buddies later in the week. Betsy coaches them as they come to multisyllabic words that they can't decode, and she also makes sure that they understand the meanings of these longer, less familiar words. When the group comes to *misunderstanding*, Sara is able to decode it. Betsy asks Sara to explain how she decoded the word successfully. Sara points to the word chunks, *mis-un-der-stand-ing*, as she says the word slowly again. Betsy asks, "What is a misunderstanding?" Tiara says, "If you don't want to do something." Betsy is supportive but adds to this for more precision. "You may not want to do something, or you may not understand something like a homework assignment, so you don't get it done on time. Friends can have a misunderstanding, too." They continue to read the story.

Teaching Vocabulary

Beck, McKeown, and Kucan (2002) discuss the importance of talking about word meanings at point of contact in a story. As the group comes to words not in their listening vocabulary while they are reading their EIR book, stop to talk about the meanings of these words. When possible, ask the children to give an approximate meaning for a word by using clues in the text. In this case, part of the discussion should focus on what clues were used to try to figure out a word meaning. However, it is important to keep in mind that using context clues is not an easy task for students; available clues may be insufficient to determine a word's meaning. If there are not sufficient context clues for an unfamiliar word in the text you are reading, tell students the word's meaning, or help them look it up in the dictionary.

See it in Action

Coaching on Vocabulary

On Day 1, Betsy coaches on word-recognition strategies, words, meanings, and comprehension. She patiently works with the students as they take turns reading parts of the story. The other students are patient, too, when Betsy stops to coach an individual. As students read, Betsy coaches them on decoding multisyllabic words, discusses the meanings of these words, discusses the meanings of potentially unfamiliar phrases in the story, and talks about what the characters are doing, how they are feeling, and why. Tiara gets stuck on the word *practicing*. Betsy asks if anyone can help, and Milan offers the word predicting. When Betsy asks them to look at the word again, Sara comes up with *practicing*. The group then works together to sound out the word *concentration*. Betsy has Tiara reread from the beginning and then finish the page. She asks, "What does it mean when George says it takes concentration to do a handstand?" Darren offers, "Like when you are taking a test." After the group has sounded out *offended*, Betsy explains how the other words in the sentence, Martha was *offended, hurt,* and *mad*, help them figure out the meaning of *offended*. Betsy and the students talk about how Martha is feeling and what *offended* means.

Day 1, Step 2: Coaching for Comprehension

(5 min.)

The notion of coaching kids for understanding should guide story discussions. In my research, I have found that limited higher-level questioning occurs in the elementary grades but a focus on high-level talk and writing about text increases students' reading abilities (Taylor et al. 2000; 2003; 2005; 2007). The purpose of coaching for comprehension is to ask questions that stretch the children's thinking and get them to think and talk about things in the story that they may not have come up with on their own. Through these prompts, students interpret the story, relate a concept in the story to their own lives, and make other connections that deepen their understanding. Since coaching for comprehension occurs on Day 2 as well, you need to remind the children that not all of them will get to answer on each day. However, if the children are eager to share their ideas, they can talk with a partner.

Examples of questions to coach for comprehension are shown in Figure 3-4. It is important to keep in mind that the questions are only examples of the kinds of questions that you might ask to stretch children's thinking about the texts they are reading.

See it iN ActioN

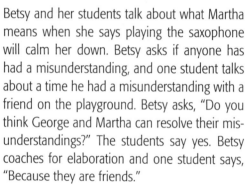

Coaching for Comprehension

Betsy and her students talk about what Martha means when she says playing the saxophone will calm her down. Betsy asks if anyone has had a misunderstanding, and one student talks about a time he had a misunderstanding with a friend on the playground. Betsy asks, "Do you think George and Martha can resolve their misunderstandings?" The students say yes. Betsy coaches for elaboration and one student says, "Because they are friends."

Often, students are able to come up with good answers when you give them sufficient wait time and offer prompts that encourage them to respond. Be sure to give students time to respond before moving on.

Day 1, Step 3: Students Reread Story
(5 min.)

On their own, students finish reading or reread the story. As children practice rereading the EIR book they will read later in the week to a first-grade child (or EIR partner), they are working on their fluency. Because they want to do a good job reading to their younger partners, they have a reason to take this practicing seriously.

Coaching for Comprehension
Questions and Prompts for Teachers

The purpose of coaching for comprehension is to *expand* students' comprehension of what they have read—rather than assess it. High-level questions are engaging, challenging, and require students to pause and think before answering.

Through Your Questioning, Students:

▶ Summarize all or part of the story or nonfiction text.

▶ Stretch their understanding of the story by asking them interpretive questions.

▶ Determine the big idea of the story, its theme.

▶ Relate the story to their lives.

▶ Discuss a big idea or theme of the story.

Examples of Questions to Coach for Comprehension

▶ Summarize the story. What happened at the beginning of the story? The middle? The end? (Answer in just a few sentences.)

▶ Why do you think Character X did Y?

▶ How did Character X change?

▶ How are you like Character X? How are you different?

▶ What did you learn from this story?

▶ What did you like or not like about this story? Why?

Interpretive Questions Based on the Text

▶ What kind of person do you think (name of character) is? What in the story makes you think this?

▶ What are some good or bad things that happen in the story? Why do you think this?

▶ What is an important thing that happened in the story? Why do you think it is important?

▶ How does (character in the story) compare to you or a family member? How is the character different?

▶ Why do you think the author gave the title he or she did to the story?

▶ What did you like best about (name a character)? Why? What in the story helped you think this way?

▶ What did you not like about (name a character)? Why? What in the story made you think this way?

▶ If you were the main character, would you have done the same things the main character did? Why or why not? What might you have done differently?

▶ Why do you think (character in the story) did . . . ?

▶ How did (character in the story) change? Why do you think this happened?

▶ What do you think were three main ideas (or most important ideas) in this article (for nonfiction)?

High-Level Questions That Relate to Children's Lives

Ask questions that are based on a concept in the story that relate to children's lives:

▶ Which character are you most like? Why?

▶ Which character would you like to be like? Why?

▶ Which character would you like most to have as a friend? Why? What in the story helped you make this decision?

▶ How are you like (character in the story)? How are you different?

▶ Can you compare anything in this story to (name another story or something else you have done in your classroom that could be compared)? Why do you think these are similar (alike) or different?

▶ Ask nonfiction-type questions that relate to your state (e.g., Could you find these animals, events in Minnesota? Why or why not? Where might they be if they could be in Minnesota?)

▶ What did you like, or not like, about this story or article (nonfiction)? Why?

Figure 3-4 Coaching for Comprehension: Questions and Prompts for Teachers

1. The teacher coaches for comprehension.

2. Together, the teacher and students complete a group sheet on summarizing a narrative story (see Figure 3-5) or answer written questions on an informational book (see Figure 3-6 for examples).

3. Children practice rereading their book as the teacher coaches individuals in word recognition, providing help with multisyllabic words.

4. The teacher explains how to use the individual take-home sheet (see Figure 3-7), which prepares students for working with their first-grade (or EIR) partner.

Day 2, Step 1: Discuss the Story and Coach for Comprehension

(3 min.)

You and your students discuss the story, and you coach for comprehension by asking them to clarify and elaborate on their ideas. This step can be brief since children will also be sharing ideas about the story on the group sheet.

ſee it iN ActioN

DAY 2
Making Connections

Betsy and her students make connections to the story they read the previous day. She asks, "What does *concentrate* mean?" Darren answers, "You have to put your mind on what you're doing." Betsy asks them to tell about a time they had to concentrate. Milan says, "Riding my bike." Betsy coaches Milan to elaborate, "How did you concentrate?" He responds, "I had to keep paying attention because I didn't want to fall." Next, Betsy asks if someone can tell about a time they felt offended like Martha did. Darren talks about a time he wanted his sister to go water skiing but she didn't want to go. Milan talks about a time when his sister ate his ice cream bar.

Day 2, Step 2: Complete a Comprehension Response Sheet Together

(12 min.)

This step varies a bit, depending on if you are reading a narrative or informational text with your students. (See Figure 3-5 for narrative text or Figure 3-6 for informational text.) On the group sheet for narrative texts, students summarize the story, make connections to the story in writing, and select and write about the meanings of two words in the story that were new to them. On the group sheet for informational text, students write answers to questions.

Summarizing a Narrative: Tips to Guide Students as They Work

One focus of the group sheet (narrative) is for children to gain skill in concisely summarizing a story, which is an important reading comprehension ability. However, often children like to go on and on retelling every detail of a story they have read. I find it helps to give them a real-word context for this task. For example, you could say to students, "If you were talking with a friend or parent about a book, how could you tell them the most important ideas about the story in just a few sentences so they wouldn't lose interest in what you were telling them?"

Remind the children of the purpose of summarizing stories, which is to concisely say in their own words the gist, or most important ideas, of the story. This is something they may need to do when they are telling their parents or a friend about a book or story they have read.

Define summarizing a story as stating the important ideas that tell what happens at the beginning (character, setting, and introduction of a problem), the middle (further events related to the problem), and the end (resolution of the problem and author's message or theme) of a story. Use these terms as you discuss the story with children so they become familiar with the idea that a summary highlights the main points of a story.

In addition to summarizing a story on Day 2, the group response sheet (Figure 3-5) has students engage in high-level thinking as they identify a part of the story they liked and make a personal connection to the story. Students also focus on vocabulary development by identifying two new words they came across in the story and providing meanings for these words through context clues, group discussion, or by looking up the definitions in the dictionary. If students do not have time to complete the sheet in the group, they can work on it at independent work time.

Teaching Strategies for Summarizing Stories

1. Model summarizing. First, talk out loud as you give a sentence or two about the beginning of the story in which you tell about the characters, setting, and the introduction of a problem. Next, give a sentence or two about the middle of the story as you tell about events that are related to the story problem. Finally, give a sentence or two about the end of the story that talks about the resolution of the problem and the theme or author's message. To make things concrete for students, write your ideas on the board as you summarize. You will need to model a few times before you coach students as they try to summarize. Even at this point, you will need to model parts of a summary as students appear to need more support.

2. Coach students as they summarize. When first beginning to work with students as they do the summarizing, ask children to give one or two sentences that tell about the beginning of the story and include the main character, the setting, and the character's problem. Get ideas from one or two children and write them on the board. Discuss which sentence(s) give summary ideas without too much detail. Also discuss how to improve upon sentences by taking out some of the details and coming up with the most important ideas for the story beginning. If necessary, model sentences that could work. Continue in the same manner to come up with a sentence or two for the middle and for the end of the story.

3. Summarizing is a difficult skill, so early in the year, there may only be time to create good summary sentences for just one part of the story. You could model sentences for the other parts of the story and have the children write them down to complete their story summary. Vary this routine in subsequent stories by having the children give summary sentences for the middle of the story while you give beginning and ending sentences, or having children give summary sentences for the ending of the story while you give sentences for the beginning and middle of a story.

4. Continue to remind children why it is so important to be able to summarize a story, to help them understand and remember the gist of the story. As you help children, point out what sentences are good summary sentences and discuss what could be left out or restated if there is too much detail.

5. If there is too much detail in a sentence, ask, "Is that a small part of the story or one of the most important ideas; for example, is it an idea that gets at the character's problem and how he solved it?" Have the child explain the answer.

6. After modeling several stories and working on sentences together, move to discussing possible ideas. Let children write their own sentences, using ideas from the discussion.

7. As children become more proficient with summarizing, have them give all of the summary sentences. They should be able to do this by the fourth or fifth story. In addition, they can write their own sentences prior to discussion and then have them share with the group the next day.

There is no right or wrong answer to sentences students generate. The goal is to work on understanding the story and how best to summarize its main points.

Summarizing Sheet for Narrative Books

Book Title: _____

Name: _____

Summarizing the Story

Tell about what you read in just one or two sentences for each part. (Be sure to include the author's message if you can.)

1. Beginning:

2. Middle:

3. End:

Share Your Ideas

1. Tell about a part you liked, or did not like, and why.

2. Make a connection to your life or the world around you.

New Words

Write two words and what they mean (by using context clues or the dictionary).

Figure 3-5   Summarizing Sheet for Narrative Books

ʃee it iN ActioN

video
5

Narrative Story Work

Betsy and her students work on a group sheet for a narrative story, engage in practice reading, and discuss the take-home sheet. Betsy works with the group on summarizing the beginning, middle, and end of the story on their group sheet. She asks them, "Do you want to tell a little detail? The whole story? Who can try to come up with a sentence for the beginning?" Darren offers, "George wanted to do handstands but Martha wanted to talk. But he had to concentrate, so he said to go away." Sara tried to summarize the middle and starts with, "She got mad." Betsy asks why. Sara adds, "George hurt her feelings." Betsy coaches, "Then what?" Sara answers, "She slammed down the phone when George called." Betsy helps Sara come up with one sentence for her ideas. Then Milan gives a sentence for the ending, "Martha played her saxophone and she felt better." Betsy gets the students to talk about a theme of the story, which is that friends have misunderstandings even though they are still friends. Betsy then tells her students to write a beginning, middle, and end for the story in their own words.

After students have written their summary, Betsy works with them on telling about a part they liked and why, telling how this story was like their own lives and why, and writing down two new words and what they each mean. Darren writes that he liked the part about handstands, and when Betsy coaches him to tell why he adds, "Because I like to do that kind of stuff."

Next, Betsy has students reread their story individually as she circulates around the group, listening and coaching as needed. Then, she briefly discusses the take-home sheet. She talks with the students about rereading their story a few times and having someone at home sign their sheet. "Don't tell me you read it 100 times because I won't believe you. If you check that you need to practice it some more, we'll find some time tomorrow to do that." They also talk about writing down one question so they can talk about their story with their first grader. She reminds them, "Let's say that last week you wrote down, *What color was the space alien's suit?* You wouldn't have had much to talk about. So what ideas do you have?" Milan offers, "Why was Martha mad at George?" Sara offers, "Why did George not want to talk to Martha?" Darren comes up with, "What happened in the beginning, middle, and end of the story?" Betsy finishes by reminding them to write down two words that they can talk about with their first grader. She talks about how *the* would not be a good word to talk about because it is hard to say what *the* means, even though it is a word that first graders can read. Betsy has students turn in their group sheets as the lesson ends.

Helping Student Write Answers to Informational Texts: Tips to Guide Students as They Work

By December you should be starting to use some of the informational books if you haven't already done so. On Day 2, students write answers to questions on these informational books. Gaetz (1991) found that children have the following problems answering questions on informational text:

1. They don't read a question carefully.

2. They don't answer all parts of a question.

3. Their answer is too general and/or too vague.

4. They tell too much detail and never state the answer precisely.

5. They just have the wrong answer.

Explaining comprehension of texts through written answers with complete and understandable responses to others is an important skill that students will use throughout their school careers. Thus, one purpose of working on written questions for informational books is to get children to read questions correctly, understand the questions, and answer all parts of multipart questions. Another purpose is to get children to answer in complete sentences. A third purpose is to help them learn how to get their thoughts down on paper in a clear yet concise manner. Sometimes, children's written answers are either too general or so long and detailed that the intent is unclear. As you and the students move to more challenging informational books, the questions should get more complex. For example, questions might ask the children to summarize the most important ideas they have read about or explain processes or concepts in these texts.

Questions for some of the exemplar grade 3 EIR books can be found in Figure 3-6. If you are using your own sets of books, you may want to use the informational question sheets provided in this book as a guide for writing your own. Note the variety of hints that accompany the questions that will help the children be successful in writing complete answers. Also, note that some of the questions do not have hints so that you and the children can check to see if they did answer questions completely. Question sheets for all of the exemplar books are in Figure 3-6 and the expanded form on the DVD.

Teaching Strategies to Help Students Write Answers to Questions for Informational Texts

To help students respond to written questions, model how to read the question carefully in order to understand what the question is asking. You might say, "If I were answering this question, first I would think, what does the question ask me to do?" It is important that children see a variety of ways to get information to answer a question.

Examples of Question Sheets for Informational Books

It's a Fruit, It's a Vegetable, It's a Pumpkin (for Fall/Winter)

Name: _____

Answer each question with a complete sentence.

1. What is a vine? Where are some places that vines can grow? (Hint: Since the question says *places*, be sure to tell more than one place a vine can grow.)
2. Summarize what you learned about the difference between a fruit and a vegetable.
3. Do you think a pumpkin is a fruit or a vegetable? Why? (Hint: Did you give a reason why?)
4. Do you like jack-o-lanterns? Why or why not?

From Seed to Plant (for Fall/Winter)

Name: _____

Answer each question with a complete sentence.

1. Explain pollination.
2. What has to happen before a seed will sprout?
3. What is a botanist? (Hint: Think about where in the book you read about this person and do a look-back.)
4. Write two sentences about a time you grew a plant. Or write two sentences about a plant you would like to grow. (Hint: Be sure to write two sentences.)

Baby Whales Drink Milk (pages 1–17) (For Winter)

Name: _____

Answer each question with a complete sentence.

1. A whale is a mammal. Name at least three other mammals. (Hint: Be sure to list three.)
2. In what ways are whales different from fish?
3. Where do humpback whales live in the summer? Where do they live in the winter? (Hint: Did you answer both questions?)
4. Summarize what you learned about baby humpback whales. (Hint: Summarize means to tell the most important ideas.)

Ocean Mammals (pages 5–31) (For Spring)

Name: _____

Answer each question with a complete sentence.

1. Name at least three ways fish and marine animals are different. (Hint: Did you give three differences?)
2. How are bottlenose and common dolphins alike? How are they different? Give at least two similarities and two differences. (Hint: Ask yourself, What is the question asking me to do?)
3. Why are manatees endangered? Give at least three reasons.
4. How have manatees been helpful to humans? Why?
5. What are two things you learned about walruses that were especially interesting?
6. Summarize the paragraph that begins at the bottom of page 42 and ends at the bottom of page 43.

Figure 3-6 Examples of Question Sheets for Exemplar Informational Books

▶ Practice a text look-back strategy. "I would try to remember where I read something that fits with the question and try to look back to this part of the book. Often, there is a key word in the question that you can search for in the text as a way to look back."

▶ Model using headings. "Sometimes the headings or titles of sections will help me to find the part where the answer is." Model finding headings and title.

▶ Model using pictures. "If the question wants me to describe something, maybe I can use a picture to help me as well as using information in the text." Show an example in a book.

▶ Model using pictures or charts to make comparisons. "If the question wants me to compare two things, maybe I can look at the pictures or at a chart."

Read through all of the questions with the students before they answer any of them. Be sure the children understand what the questions are asking. Model a strategy you would use to find the answer or ask one of the children what they would do.

You will need to coach students when they have incorrect or partially incorrect answers. Here are some suggestions for teaching strategies that will help students improve their written answers to questions.

▶ Coach children when they write responses that are too general. Example: Why do some people like oil and natural gas better than coal? Answer: *Oil and natural gas get around better.* Coach on how to elaborate on this answer: *Of course, oil and natural gas don't get around by themselves. How else can you say this?* Second attempt: *Oil and natural gas can be moved more easily than coal, like in a pipeline.*

▶ Coach children when they don't answer all parts of a question. Example: What are two reasons people like oil and natural gas better than coal? Answer: *Coal is harder to move.* Coach on how to reread the question and answer it completely: *That is one good answer, but what does the question ask for?* Coach: *Look for the key words* oil *and* natural gas *and reread to find a second reason.* Second attempt: *Coal is harder to move and oil and natural gas are cleaner than coal when they burn.*

▶ Coach when a child rambles on with an answer and needs to be more focused in the response. Example: Why have we needed more energy in the past 150 years? Answer: *Because of stuff like machines, and lamps, and telephones, and TVs, and cars.* Coach: *You are on the right track. But how can you say it without just listing five examples. Also, remember to use a complete sentence. Maybe start with "People," and talk about inventions.* Second attempt: *People have been coming up with inventions like machines and cars that use a lot of energy, so we need more energy.*

▶ Coach children when they have the wrong answer. Start by having them look back in the text. A key word in the question may help them find a section of the text to look at again. Tell them to think about where this key word is in the passage, and to look there to work on the answer. Have them reread and then ask questions to guide them to a more appropriate response. They may have to put ideas together across two or more sentences.

The answer may not be explicitly stated in just one sentence. Example: Before the 1800s, what types of energy were used to do work? Answer: *Steam.* Coach: *I think you need to look back in the text. Look for the key term* 1800s *and reread for types of energy that were used before the 1800s to get work done. Remember to use a complete sentence.* Second attempt: *Before the 1800s, people used types of energy like their hands, animals, and windmills or waterfalls to get work done.* In this example, the answer was spread across three sentences in the text. Also, students had to look at the picture of a watermill in the text and perhaps use background knowledge to come up with *waterfalls* as a source of energy since the text only said that energy from water turned a wheel that ground grain.

At the beginning of the year, children will probably not be able to answer all the questions during the EIR lesson, but it is good practice for them to answer all of them at some time over a day or two. This can be done in several ways: have the children answer a number of questions in writing and then do the rest orally, have students do the questions over a two-day period, let students work with partners, or have them work on them during independent work time. As the year progresses, however, it is a good idea to get each child to answer all of the questions in writing. When you discuss answers with students, continue to ask them how they came up with them.

Day 2, Step 3: Students Practice Fluent Reading and Prepare for Tutoring

(5 min.)

Often, children like to read their EIR book to a partner on Day 2. They can practice coaching as one or the other gets stuck on a word, just as they will have to coach their first-grade reader when they read their EIR story later in the week. However, if they are not working with first graders, you would skip this step as they will do EIR partner reading on Day 3.

Day 2, Step 4: Discuss Take-Home Sheet

(5 min.)

In addition to practicing at school, children should take their book home for additional practice on Day 2. Teachers report that they have little trouble getting the children to return their books because they know they need to have them on Day 4 to read to their first-grade partner.

At home, the children complete the individual take-home sheet (Figure 3-7). In addition to practicing their story and writing down how many times they read it, students write one question on the sheet and two vocabulary words to discuss with their first grader (or EIR partner). A parent or guardian signs the take-home sheet to acknowledge that the work was done.

Individual Take-Home Sheet

Book Title: _____

Name: _____ **Parent Signature:** _____

Reading for Fluency

I practiced my story _____times.

_____ I am ready to read it to my first grader (or EIR partner).

_____ I need to practice some more.

Discussion

Write down one question about the story that makes you think and that you and your partner can discuss.

New Words

Write down two words to ask or tell your first grader (or EIR partner) about (and what they mean).

Word 1

Word 2

© 2010 by Barbara M. Taylor from *Catching Readers, Grade 3*. Portsmouth, NH: Heinemann.

Figure 3-7 Individual Take-Home Sheet

1. The teacher discusses the take-home sheet, which is used to help prepare students for working with their first-grade partner. (Or, the teacher checks sheets and discusses them with individual students as needed before they use them in Step 4 on Day 3 with an EIR partner.) You should have students complete this sheet on Day 3 if it is not sent home.

2. Students practice reading the EIR first-grade book (if available) so they are sure they can successfully coach their first-grade partner.

3. The teacher and students discuss strategies for coaching first graders.

4. Students practice reading their grade 3 EIR book if they indicate on their take-home sheet that they need more practice The teacher can conduct an oral reading analysis (see Chapter 4) or and oral reading fluency check (see Chapter 5) at this time.

However, if the cross-age tutoring piece is not in place, have EIR partners coach one another as they take turns reading their story and use their take-home sheets to discuss vocabulary and talk about the story.

Day 3, Step 1: Review Take-Home Sheet
(5 min.)

First, review students' take-home sheets with them. Check to see that they have written a question to ask their first grader (or EIR partner) that will generate some discussion. Also make sure that they have selected vocabulary words that can be explained and that are not too easy or too difficult for their first grader (or EIR partner) to talk about with them.

ſee it iN ActioN

video 6

DAY 3
Preparing for Partner Reading

Betsy begins the Day 3 lesson by asking students about rereading their EIR story at home. "I want to know if you feel you are ready to read to your first grader tomorrow." Students report on how many times they read their *George and Martha* story and say they are ready to read aloud to their first-grade partner the next day. Betsy also asks them to share their discussion questions. Students offer, "Why did Martha decide to call George? What did you like in the story and why?" Betsy compliments this student for adding why. A third student gives her questions, "Why did Martha get mad?" Betsy coaches, "You might also ask, *What would you do?*, so you have a little more to talk about with your first grader." Students also share their vocabulary words: *misunderstanding, hope, saxophone.* Betsy reminds her group, "Put your sheets in the back of your books so you don't lose them. You'll need them tomorrow."

Day 3, Step 2: Students Read Grade 1 EIR Story
(5 min.)

If at all possible, it is important to borrow copies of the EIR books the first graders will be reading to the third graders so the older children have a chance to practice reading these books. You don't want them to be in the uncomfortable position of not knowing a particular word and being expected to coach their younger partner. Teachers report that their third graders often have trouble reading the grade 1 story without practicing it first.

Day 3, Step 3: Review Coaching Strategies
(5 min.)

Discuss strategies for coaching the first graders (or EIR partners). Teachers have found a sheet with prompts for partner reading works well. (See Figure 3-8.) As an alternative, some teachers have the children generate their own list of coaching prompts. Also, you want the students to understand that if their first grader gets stuck, they should give a hint or two before they tell the child the word.

Prompts for Partner Reading

"It starts with _____."
(child gives his reading partner the beginning sound)

"This part says _____."
(child provides his partner with a rhyming part like *at* or *op*)

"Look at the picture . . ."

"Look at this word again . . ."
(if child who is reading misreads a word)

"Break it into chunks"
(if partner is a grade 3 EIR student.)

Figure 3-8 Prompts for Partner Reading

During the fall, the third-grade students are sometime disappointed that the first-grade students don't need much coaching as they read their EIR stories. This is because the grade 1 EIR stories are very short in the fall and the younger children may have memorized them. Just point this out to your students and let them know that as the year goes on, the first graders' stories will get harder and so the younger children will need more help.

It is also important to discuss with the third graders strategies for keeping the younger children interested as they are reading aloud to them. For example, if a younger child is not paying attention, they may need to ask a question to get their partner focused again on the story, or they may ask about a picture to draw them back in.

ſee it iN ActioN

video 7

Strategies for Partner Reading

This video clip shows third graders discussing strategies for coaching first graders. Students read the first-grade story with no mistakes. Then, Betsy has them look at the word *wake* toward the end of the story. She asks, "What would you do if your student said *woke* instead of *wake*? What kind of clue could you give?" Sara says she could give the /w/ sound. Tiara says, "Tell her it's a long *a*." Alex adds, "Tell her it's a silent *e* at the end." They also discuss the word, *television*. Alex says he would break it into parts for his first-grade partner. Betsy says that might work but it also might be too hard for a first grader and asks for other ideas. Tiara says she would tell her partner it was a longer word for TV. Betsy tells them these are all good ideas and adds, "It's hard to not give them the word, but we want to get them to think for themselves."

Day 3, Step 4: Rereading Grade 3 Selection

(5 min.)

Give students a chance to reread their grade 3 EIR story or nonfiction text one more time. It is important to save a few minutes of the lesson for this if some of the students indicated on their take-home sheet that they needed additional time to practice. If students do reread their stories, you can do an oral reading analysis (see Chapter 4) or an oral reading fluency check (see Chapter 5) on one student at this time.

If the cross-age tutoring piece is not in place, have EIR partners coach one another as they take turns reading their story. They should use the coaching prompts in Figure 3-8 if a partner gets suck on a word. They then use their take-home sheets to discuss vocabulary and talk about the story.

See it iN ActioN

Prereading for Partner Reading

In this video clip we see grade 3 students reading through the grade 1 EIR book that they will be listening to, and coaching, as their first-grade partners read.

Day 4
Lesson Routine

1. Third graders read their story to first-grade partners. (Remember to spend two days on Day 5 instead if the cross-age tutoring piece is not in place).

2. Third graders work with first graders on comprehension and vocabulary from ideas on their individual take-home sheets.

3. Third graders listen to first graders read their EIR story and coach as needed.

On Day 4, the third graders work with their first-grade partners for 20 minutes. Each time the pair is the same. In this way, friendships begin to build. Once in a while, a pair just doesn't seem to be a good match, and changes will need to be made if this happens.

Most teachers find it works best if they work with one first-grade teacher on the partner reading. Usually, the third graders go to the first-grade classroom to work with the younger children, but you may find some other arrangement works well. The older children need an adult (e.g., educational assistant, parent or grandparent volunteer) in the room who can provide help if problems arise. They may need to be reminded to coach, not tell, when the younger child gets stuck on a word. They may need to be offered a suggestion to get a child back on track if he is not paying attention during the older student's read aloud.

see it in Action

DAY 4
Partner Reading

In this video segment we see third-grade EIR students (from a different school than Betsy's) read with their first-grade EIR buddies. First, the third graders read their stories, ask their question, and talk about the vocabulary words they selected. Then they listen to their first-grade partners read their EIR stories and coach as needed.

Third-grade teachers report that they learn how to help their students be good tutors if they watch the tutoring sessions on occasion. If your third graders go to a first-grade classroom, I recommend that you work with your principal to arrange to get coverage in your classroom so that you can attend these tutoring sessions.

Often teachers say they are already engaged in cross-age partner reading with their entire class and another entire class. If this is the case, I recommend that the EIR cross-age tutoring be a second opportunity for the EIR children to work with a younger child. In this way, their EIR tutoring is seen as something special and, consequently, motivating for them.

Lesson Routine

1. The teacher and students discuss the partner reading experience from the previous day. They talk about things that went well, share problems, and talk about solutions to problems.

2. There are several activities to choose from for Step 2. Using a grade-level text, the teacher and students read a short selection and focus on attacking multisyllabic words, discuss vocabulary, summarize, and generate and answer thought-provoking comprehension questions.

   Or, students engage in independent reading as the teacher conducts an oral reading analysis or oral reading fluency check on one or more students.

   Or, the teacher assesses students' abilities to write summaries for short texts not read before or to write answers to high-level thinking and comprehension strategy questions on these texts.

Day 5, Step 1: Debriefing on the Tutoring Session
{5 min.}

Teachers have learned over the years that it is important to provide support to their third graders in terms of working with a younger student. One way to do this is by having a discussion the day following the tutoring. For example, students might comment on successes, "My partner is reading better and learning longer words. I read with expression so my grade 1 partner pays attention." Questions might focus on problems such as: "What can I do when my partner doesn't listen to me? What should I do if my partner is moving around?"

Day 5, Step 2: Give Students Additional Reading Practice with Additional Texts
(15 min.)

I recommend that the tutoring be on Day 4 because three days is long enough to spend on one story and to get the children ready to read to their younger partners. However, because the grade 3 EIR children are in the program to receive extra support in reading, I also recommend that they get the chance on Day 5 (or Days 4 and 5 if the cross-age tutoring component is not in place) to work on word attack, vocabulary, and comprehension related to a grade-level text, such as their basal reader or social studies text. This reading should be done silently so the children practice reading in this mode. Ask students to jot down words they come across in their reading that they don't know how to decode or words that they don't know the meanings of. Discuss these words after students have read the text segment you have selected for them. Additionally, the teacher or students can summarize a section of their grade-level text and generate discussion questions that will stretch the children's thinking.

If you do not wish to do this additional reading from a grade-level textbook, you should still meet to discuss the previous day of tutoring with the children. One thing teachers have done in the past is to have children write in a journal about their tutoring session with their first-grade buddy and then use what they have written as a basis for a discussion about their experiences.

Following the debriefing discussion, another alternative on Day 5 is to have the children read a book for pleasure, as opposed to reading from a textbook, for the remainder of the 20-minute EIR session. During this time, you can conduct an oral reading analysis (see Chapter 4) or an oral reading fluency check (see Chapter 5) on one or more students.

One other assessment activity you can do on Day 5 a few times a year is to have students write summaries for short texts or to write answers to high-level thinking and comprehension strategy questions using passages they have not read before. You can use the scoring rubrics described in Chapter 5 to monitor students' progress on these two types of reading comprehension tasks.

EIR Book Selection Guides and Other Lesson-Planning Resources

Providing students with quality children's literature to read is an essential piece of effective instruction, and every EIR lesson relies on an engaging book. In this section, I give you guidance on how to select good books for the EIR model. However, I want to emphasize that you need to make your own choices and discoveries about the fiction and nonfiction books you use in EIR lessons. Why? Because somehow, following anyone else's suggestions flattens the vitality of the teaching and learning. Go with your own expertise, interests, and the curiosities and sense of humor of your students.

The books you use should be written on a second- to easy-third-grade level and also appeal to the first-grade students to whom your third-grade students will read. Here are more guidelines to consider:

▶ Select about five or six picture books that can be read to a first-grade EIR student in about 10 to 15 minutes.

▶ Select four or five easy readers that you can break into two parts and spend two weeks on each book. If the narrative books are too long to read in one or two weeks, work with your students on how to select part of a book to read aloud, and perhaps another part to tell about, before moving on to the questioning and vocabulary activities that go along with the narrative books.

▶ Select about ten informational books that you can break into two parts and spend two weeks on each part. If your students are not able to read everything in the informational books to their first-grade buddies due to time constraints, you can work with them on selecting the parts that they will read aloud.

In Table 3-1 and on the DVD, you will find an exemplar book list that will help guide you as you look for certain characteristics when choosing books for EIR. This list will assist your planning and carrying out the lesson steps. Remember, you do not need to use the books that are given; they are just examples. However, to get you started, I've also provided questions with hints for exemplar EIR informational books (see Figure 3-1 and expanded Figure 3-6 on the DVD). I hope that by seeing what is done with the exemplar books, you will have a better idea of how to write questions for the informational books you choose to use for EIR lessons.

Additional resources that will help you teach EIR lessons are available in the Appendices on the DVD. Materials include teaching charts, an open-ended group sheet for narrative books, examples of questions for informational books, an individual take-home sheet, examples of independent activities for all students, and assessment directions and recording forms. Some of these resources were discussed in this chapter; others are described in Chapters 4 and 5.

Summary of the Five-Day Routine

Now that we have covered the basic grade 3 EIR procedures, we'll turn to a few other instructional strategies that support these daily lessons in Chapter 4. We'll also take a look at how to implement comprehension strategy instruction with students using informational text if you feel they are ready for new challenges by January or later in the school year.

DISCUSS WITH YOUR COLLEAGUES

1. Discuss the video clips you saw and the teachers' use of coaching to help children respond, regardless of whether the focus was on word recognition, vocabulary, or comprehension.

2. Discuss ways in which you might set up the cross-age tutoring between third and first graders in EIR.

Additional Instructional Strategies

• •

To meet your third graders' individual needs in EIR, you draw from your own teaching experiences, your instincts about the child, as well as the content of the lesson procedures described in the previous chapter. In this chapter, I highlight some additional teaching strategies for you to consider if you need to provide a child with additional support in word recognition or if you want to provide your students with new challenges by teaching them a sequence of comprehension strategies to use with informational or narrative texts.

One-on-One Reading with a Volunteer or Educational Assistant

For students who are struggling with word recognition, have them read their EIR story or nonfiction text once a week with an adult who has received training on how to coach in word recognition. This one-on-one reading should be done as early in the week as possible when the book is still a challenge to the student; by the end of the week they will have read the selection multiple times and the reading of the selection will be much easier for them and they will not need as much coaching support. This opportunity to read one-on-one with a coach also gives students the chance to practice decoding and reading with fluency in a relaxed environment. More discussion of one-on one-coaching and how to provide training to the adults serving in this role is in Chapter 7.

Oral Reading Analysis and Instruction

If you have students who are still struggling with word recognition, begin oral reading analysis with them (Taylor et al. 1995). You can do this on Day 3 or 5. In an oral reading analysis, you take three, 100-word samples of a student's reading of material at his or her instructional level (92–97 percent accuracy in word recognition). This material should be texts read "cold," or not read before by the student. The multiple readings can be spread out over a week to ten days. You analyze these samples to determine one problem area to focus on and provide instruction. As the student does subsequent oral readings, you continue to assess in this focus area, monitoring with a progress chart to document the student's growth in the target area. Once the student has made good progress in one problem area, move to another as needed. Potential problem areas and recommendations for instruction follow. The procedures for oral reading analysis are described next in Figures 4-1 and 4-2, and a chart you can use to take notes when you conduct oral reading analysis is in Figure 4-3.

Recording Errors for Oral Reading Analysis

1. The following is an example of a child's reading of a story, marked as an oral reading analysis (What the child read is in parentheses; words in bold are the actual words in the text.) Note that the child has read this story with 94 percent accuracy, so it is at the appropriate level for oral reading analysis. *SC* is used to indicate a self-correction and is not counted as an error. *SD* is used to indicate a word the student had to stop on to decode, but the student was successful in coming up with the word without even making a self-correction.

    Once upon a time, a man lived in a **hut** (house) with this mother, his wife, and six children. It was very crowded and **noisy** (nosy) in the hut. So the man went to see the **wiseman** (wiseman—SD). The wiseman told him to put his **chickens** (chicks), goat, and cow in

Oral Reading Analysis

Type of Error and Problem/Instruction and Ongoing Assessment

Type of Error or Problem	Instruction/Assessment
Analysis. Student doesn't know how to break a long word into chunks and blend those chunks together.	This is the word-recognition problem that is the hardest to correct. Continue to use the decoding multisyllabic words strategy discussed in Chapter 3. Continue to model for a student how to break a word into chunks. Continue to coach a student to use the decoding multisyllabic words strategy himself to figure out hard words. Keep a progress chart of the number of times a student at least tried to figure out a hard word, or the number of time a student was successful figuring it out.
Automatic. Student makes an error automatically; that is, the word comes out almost instantly, but it is the wrong word.	At the end of the page, ask the student if he knows what word he read very quickly but read incorrectly. If he does not, reread the sentence the way he read it as he reads along, and ask again. Typically, when a student sees what he is doing, he begins to read more carefully and makes fewer automatic errors.
Meaning. Student makes an error that doesn't make sense.	At the end of a page, ask the student to identify which word in the sentence didn't make sense as he read it. If the student doesn't know, reread it for him as he read it. Have him try to figure out the correct word, paying particular attention to the meaning of the text. Keep a progress chart of the number of times the student self-corrected an error that didn't make sense. Typically, once this problem is brought to the student's attention, the number of errors self-corrected goes up quite readily.
Basic sight word. Student makes an error with a basic sight words.	This is a problem if it is frequent. Often a student doesn't believe he is doing this since he knows the words in isolation. Reread the sentence where the basic sight word was read incorrectly, and ask the child to tell you what word was incorrect. Talk about the problem of reading so quickly that errors are made. Again, once the student sees what she is doing, she is usually able to fairly readily correct this problem.
Omission. Student skips over a hard word.	This is a problem if it is frequent. Often students skip words because they don't know how to attack multisyllabic words. Use the suggestions in Chapter 3 to help them with this strategy. Be sure to praise a child when he does not skip over words but works at breaking them into chunk when necessary.

© 2010 by Barbara M. Taylor from *Catching Readers, Grade 3*. Portsmouth, NH: Heinemann.

Figure 4-1 Oral Reading Analysis

Additional Instructional Strategies   **61**

the hut. The man did as he was told. Now it became very, very crowded and **noisy** (noise—SC) in the hut. The man was **exasperated** (experated), so he went back to see the wiseman. The wiseman told him to take the animals out of the hut. The man did as he was told. **Finally** (finally with short *i*), it **did** (does) not seem crowded and noisy in the hut **anymore** (anymore—SD), and the man and his family lived happily (happy) ever after.

COMMENTS ON ERRORS IN SAMPLE

hut (house): The child instantly came out with *house* and didn't self-correct.

noisy (nosy): The child instantly came out with *nosy*, but it clearly doesn't make sense in the story. Note that this error is counted as both an automatic error and a meaning error.

chickens (chicks): The child instantly came out with *chicks* and didn't self-correct.

noisy (noise—SC): This time the child read *noise* for *noisy* but then self-corrected. This is not counted as an error.

exasperated (experated): The child did not pronounce the second syllable so this is marked as an error involving an analysis difficulty. In this case, it was probably due to the fact that the child did not recognize, or even know, the word *exasperated*. However, *experated* did not make sense, and the child should have taken a closer look at the word. Notice that this error was marked as both an error involving analysis and meaning.

finally (finally with short *i*): The child read the word with the short vowel sound instead of the long vowel sound. This is marked as a meaning error since the nonword doesn't make sense. Note that the error isn't marked as an analysis error since all of the sounds in the word are represented. The sound given for the *i* is the wrong sound. It is also not marked as an automatic error, which indicates that the child did not instantly come out with the wrong pronunciation for the word.

did (does): The child automatically came out with *does* for *did*. Since *did* is a basic sight word, this is noted under column 5.

anymore—SD: The child paused on this word because he didn't instantly recognize it. However, when he did say something for the word, it was the correct word. This is not counted as an error.

happily (happy): The child instantly came out with *happy* and didn't self-correct. It is not marked as an analysis error since the child didn't even take time to analyze it, but automatically came out with the wrong word.

Oral Reading Analysis
Sample of a Completed Recording Chart

1 Error	2 Analysis Difficulty	3 Automatic Error	4 Meaning Error	5 Other Errors (basic sight words, phonic elements, omissions)	6 Notes
hut (house)		X			
noisy (nosy)		X	X	Gave long *o* for *oi*	Teacher tells the child the word to get him back on track.
chickens (chicks)		X			
noisy (noise—SC)					
exasperated (experated)	X		X		
finally (finally with short *i*)			X	Gave short *i* instead of long *i*.	
did (does)		X		Basic sight word error— gave *does* but word was *did*	
anymore (SD)					Student has a long pause and then comes up with the word
happily (happy)		X			

Key to Columns in Chart

1   **Error.** This is an error (unless it is marked as SC or SD) due to the substitution of a real word or nonword for the actual word. The student's substitution should be written above the actual word. (*SC* is used to indicate a self-correction. *SD* is used to indicate a word the student had to stop on to decode, but the student was successful in coming up with the word without even making a self-correction. Neither of these are counted as errors when writing in a book or on a sheet.)

2   **Error Due to Analysis Difficulty.** The student does not seem to be able to work through the entire word but is only able to decode part of it. Error is marked with an X in column 2.

3   **Automatic Error.** The student quickly reads the word so that it comes out automatically. However, the word is not read correctly. Error is marked with an X in column 3.

4   **Meaning Error.** The student comes up with a real word or nonword that really doesn't make sense in the context of the text being read. Error is marked with an X in column 4. Be somewhat liberal here. For example, I would not count *house* for *hut, chicks* for *chickens,* or *happy* for *happily* as meaning errors because I want to especially focus on instances in which the meaning is seriously impaired. (However, this involves personal judgment and I realize that some would want to count *house* for *hut* as a meaning error. I just tell teachers to try to be consistent in how they score errors.)

5   **Other Errors.** Here you list other errors such as those in which the student gave the wrong sound for a letter or letters (wrong phonic element), the student misread a basic sight word, or the student omitted a word. For omissions, write the word column 5 in and circle it.

6   **Notes.** In this column you can write down comments about an error or successfully decoded word or other thoughts you have about the student's reading behaviors during the oral reading.

Figure 4-2   Oral Reading Analysis Sample

Focus for Instruction

First, it would be best to look across three samples before making a decision about where to focus in terms of instruction. Also, this is a personal decision. There is no right answer about where to focus first. However, because five of the child's seven errors were automatic errors, I would be inclined to begin with this first as my focus. After a child has shown improvement in this area, I would focus on helping the child correct errors that didn't make sense.

Oral Reading Analysis Recording Sheet

1 Error (or SC/SD word)	2 Analysis Difficulty	3 Automatic Error	4 Meaning Error	5 Other Errors (basic sight words, phonic elements, omissions)	6 Notes

Figure 4-3 Blank Oral Reading Analysis Recording Sheet

Strategies for Informational Text (January–May)

The Reciprocal Teaching Model

If you think your students are ready for a new challenge by January or later, you may want to try the reciprocal teaching model with them for the last few months of school. In this model, children work in a group as they go through the steps of asking important questions, summarizing, clarifying confusions, and predicting as a way to read and study informational texts, including textbooks they will be asked to read on their own in social studies and science.

The reciprocal teaching model was developed by Palincsar and Brown (1984, 1986) for middle-grade students who could decode grade-level informational but not comprehend it well. A considerable amount of research has found the technique to be effective in improving students' reading comprehension (Rosenshine and Meister 1994; NRP 2000). The model can be explained to students as a study strategy, or as a way to help them learn to study and to glean the most important ideas from informational text. The children work in a group as they carry out four procedures, or steps of the reciprocal teaching model, with chunks of text. Students take turns being the "teacher" for a chunk. This aspect of the model has great appeal to children. The reciprocal teaching model is discussed below. (Also see Figure 4-4.)

If you think the reciprocal teaching model would be too advanced for your students, I recommend that you still focus during the last few months of school on children's reading and comprehension of informational books. Without using the complete reciprocal teaching model, you can help children work on summarizing the key ideas of a page or so of text in only two to three sentences. You can also work with them on comprehension monitoring (i.e., knowing that what they read has to make sense, and if it does not, going back and trying a fix-up strategy). To work on summarizing alone, see instructional suggestions in Figure 4-5. To work on comprehension monitoring alone, see the discussion of clarifying confusions as part of the reciprocal teaching procedures described next.

When teaching students to use the reciprocal teaching model, at first the chunks of text should be about as long as a paragraph. That is, students should go through the four steps of the model one paragraph at a time. After two to three weeks of this, however, the children should move on to working with larger chunks, such as a page or a section (several paragraphs) of text at a time.

The children will need you to model how to come up with important questions, how to summarize, and how to clarify anything that is confusing. Over time, however, you will be able to release responsibility to the children for these tasks and assume the role of a coach who provides support.

Reciprocal Teaching Model Steps

▶ Ask one to two important questions about the chunk of text and get answers.

▶ Summarize the important ideas of the chunk in two to three sentences.

▶ Clarify anything that is confusing (practice comprehension monitoring).

▶ Make any predictions (if they come to mind) about what will be read next.

Figure 4-4 Reciprocal Teaching Model Steps

Asking Important Questions

Children find it easier to come up with important questions if they try to ask a question that starts with "how" or "why." If they ask "what," "where," or "when" questions, I tell them to be sure that their question is about a big idea and not a minor detail.

Summarizing

I have found that children will be more successful with summarizing if the number of sentences they can use in their summary is limited. For a paragraph, I would tell them to come up with one sentence that is more than an "about" sentence (e.g., *It is about . . .*) and that tells the most important thing they think the author was trying to communicate in the paragraph.

For several paragraphs, a page, or a section of text, I would ask them to tell the most important ideas the author was trying to get across in just two to three sentences (depending on the length of the chunk).

Summarizing is a very difficult task for children and they will need a lot of practice with this process. One reason that summarizing is so difficult for children is that they do not look at text the same way an adult does. Often, what is important to them is what is most colorful or interesting. However, by third grade, students need to start to learn from reading informational text. This requires learning how to understand and summarize the most important ideas an author is trying to get across. For more on summarizing informational text, see Figure 4-5.

Clarifying Confusions

With this step, students are really practicing comprehension monitoring. That is, when something doesn't make sense, the reader should notice this and do something about it because the purpose of reading is to understand the text. By modeling comprehension monitoring, you are helping the students see that not only is it okay, but it is normal for a reader to be confused by things when reading.

Children, especially struggling readers, often have a hard time learning to notice and stop when something isn't making sense. Often, for struggling readers, this is because they have not learned to read for meaning, or expect meaning to come from the act of reading, to the extent that they should.

Once children learn to notice that something isn't making sense, they need to learn a few fix-up strategies to improve their comprehension. One fix-up strategy is to simply reread. Another is to ask a question about what is confusing, and then reread, trying to answer the question. Another is to see if there is a word that you don't understand, and if there is, use context clues or the dictionary to come up with the meaning of the word (or approximate meaning in the case of context clues). A fourth strategy is to see if you haven't decoded a long word correctly and to use the decoding multisyllabic words strategy described in Chapter 3 to figure out the word.

Instructional Suggestions for Summarizing Informational Text

▶ First, explain to the students that summarizing means being able to list or explain the most important ideas contained in a paragraph, a page, or a section of text. Tell them it is impossible to remember all the ideas in informational text so it is important to learn how to remember and identify the most important ideas.

▶ Model how to read one paragraph, page, or section of informational text at a time and select two or three words from the paragraph, page, or section that reflects its topic. These are "about statements" (e.g., "This page was about elephant teeth.").

▶ Model (talk aloud) how to turn the "about statement" into a complete sentence that reflects the most important idea. Write the idea on the board. This is a main idea sentence.

▶ If a page or section is used, write down one to three other important ideas.

▶ Students have a tendency to write too many ideas so it is important they learn how to limit the number of ideas. Ask, "What do you think are the most important ideas the author wanted you to remember?"

▶ Model to explain why certain ideas would not be good main idea sentences because they are too general or too specific or not that important.

▶ Repeat this process for a few more sections, until they are able to do a three-to-five-page reading.

▶ Finally, model how to study from the written summary by reading it over and reciting the important ideas.

▶ Repeat the above process as much as needed before the students write their own summary statements.

▶ For guided practice, the teacher and students work together through several sections of text, summarizing in the manner specified above while the teacher provides support as necessary.

▶ For independent practice, the students work alone or with a partner to summarize a section or two from the text and then practice studying their summary.

Figure 4-5 *Instructional Suggestions for Summarizing Informational Text*

> ❱ Reread.

> ❱ Ask yourself a question about what is confusing you and reread to answer your question.

> ❱ Use context clues or the dictionary to figure out the meaning of a word you don't know.

> ❱ Use the strategy for decoding multisyllabic words on a long word you think you have not decoded correctly.

Making Predictions

This step can be optional. I recommend that students make a prediction about what they will read next if it comes to mind, but they do not need to force the making of predictions.

READ ABOUT IT IN ACTION AND LEARN MORE

To read about reciprocal teaching in action, you can turn to Appendix 2-1 and Chapter 2. In Appendix 2-1 on the DVD, Karen Olsen reviews reciprocal teaching strategies with her students in a whole group lesson and in guided reading groups. In Chapter 2, there is a short description of a group of advanced readers in Karen's class practicing reciprocal teaching strategies as part of a book club discussion on *The Sign of the Beaver.* Also, to learn more about teaching students to use reciprocal teaching strategies, see Oczkus (2003).

Summary

Now that we have focused on instructional strategies to use with grade 3 students who need additional reading support, we turn to assessments. In Chapter 5, you will learn about initial assessments to determine those students who will benefit from EIR lessons, ongoing assessments to help you evaluate students' progress and make adjustments to instruction, and assessments at the end of the year to help you determine students' reading abilities as they complete third grade.

DISCUSS WITH YOUR COLLEAGUES

1. Discuss ways in which you could build oral reading analysis into your teaching repertoire.

2. Ask one another questions and discuss the pros and cons of teaching your students to use reciprocal teaching strategies. Share experiences with this technique.

Assessing Third Graders in EIR

I n this chapter, I share fall and spring assessments that will help you determine which third graders will benefit from supplemental reading instruction as well as provide advice for monitoring their reading progress throughout the year.

Fall Assessments

In September, assess third graders who appear to be reading below grade level to see if they would benefit from the supplemental EIR instruction. These assessments are typical of the kinds of classroom-based assessments teachers give their students at the beginning of the school year. If you have required assessments that give you the same information as described in this chapter, you can use them instead. All assessments are administered individually, and they are best given in the morning when children are less tired, as opposed to in the afternoon. Other children can be working on independent reading activities during this time.

Use an informal reading inventory (e.g., Qualitative Reading Inventory 4 by Leslie and Caldwell 2006) to determine which students need the grade 3 EIR program. Directions for administering portions of this test for the purposes of EIR placement are provided in Figure 5-1. A summarizing scoring rubric to assess comprehension (Figure 5-2) and a fall summary sheet to record scores (Figure 5-3) can also be found on the DVD.

Directions for Grade 3 Fall Assessment

Oral reading: Errors include substitutions, omissions, teacher-assisted or teacher-pronounced words. Self-corrections, repetitions, proper names, or hesitations are *not* errors. If the child mispronounces the same word more than once, count each mispronunciation as an error.

Step 1. Have the student read a grade 1 passage for one minute. Put a check mark above each word read incorrectly (error). If a student is stuck on a word in this 1-minute timed reading, wait about five seconds, then tell the student the word. Mark the last word read in the minute.

Step 2. Have the student continue to read the passage to the end as you mark errors made. Now that you are no longer timing the student, use your own judgment on time before telling a word, but again give about five second time wait. Stop if the child is reading at less than 90 percent word recognition accuracy on the grade 1 informal reading inventory (IRI) passage (see Step 6), and do not do the summarizing or comprehension questions (continue to Steps 5 and 6).

Step 3. Ask the student to summarize the selection. Use the four-point rubric to score as shown on the Summarizing Rubric (see Figure 5-2). Record score 1, 2, 3, or 4 on the fall summary sheet. (See Figure 5-3.)

Step 4. Ask the student questions about the passage. Record the number and percent of questions answered correctly on the summary sheet.

Step 5. Go back and count the number of words read correctly in one minute. Record on summary sheet.

Step 6. Calculate word-recognition accuracy. This is the number of words read correctly (total number of words in passage minus errors) divided by the total number of words). Record on summary sheet.

If not already done, transfer all information to Fall Summary Sheet (see Figure 5-3). If the student reads the grade 1 passage with above 90 percent accuracy in word recognition, continue to the grade 2 passage and repeat Steps 1–6. Stop if the child is below 90 percent accuracy and do not do the summarizing or comprehension questions (continue to Steps 5 and 6).

If student reads the grade 2 passage with 92 percent accuracy or above in word recognition, continue to grade 3 passage and repeat Steps 1 through 6. If the child is below 90 percent accuracy, do not do the summarizing or comprehension questions (continue to Steps 5 and 6) and stop.

Figure 5-1 Directions for Fall Assessment

Summarizing Rubric

Passage _____ Child's Name _____

Summarizing: Say, *"Summarize the most important ideas you just read about."*

> **Record student's response as best as possible:**

Score:

Scoring Guide:

1	2	3	4
▶ Student offers little or no information about the selection. ▶ Summary is incomprehensible. ▶ Stated ideas do not relate to the selection.	▶ Student relates details only. ▶ Student is unable to recall the gist of the selection. ▶ Summary is incomplete or ideas are misconstrued.	▶ Student relates some main ideas and some supporting details. ▶ Summary is fairly coherent.	▶ All major points and appropriate supporting details are included. ▶ High degree of completeness and coherence. ▶ Student generalizes beyond the text.

Figure 5-2 Summarizing Rubric Sheet

See the DVD for full-size versions of all the forms in this chapter.

Grade 3 Fall Summary Sheet

Grade 3	Grade 1 passage from an informal reading inventory					Grade 2 passage from an informal reading inventory				
Student	Words Correct in First Minute	Number of Errors in Total Passage	Word-Recognition Accuracy (Percent Correct)	Summary Score (4-Point Rubric)	Questions Correct (Percent)	Words Correct in First Minute	Number of Errors in Total Passage	Word-Recognition Accuracy (Percent Correct)	Summary Score (4-Point Rubric)	Questions Correct (Percent)

Grade 3	Grade 3 passage from an informal reading inventory					Extra grade ____ passage from an informal reading inventory				
Student	Words Correct in First Minute	Number of Errors in Total Passage	Word-Recognition Accuracy (Percent Correct)	Summary Score (4-Point Rubric)	Questions Correct (Percent)	Words Correct in First Minute	Number of Errors in Total Passage	Word-Recognition Accuracy (Percent Correct)	Summary Score (4-Point Rubric)	Questions Correct (Percent)

Figure 5-3 Fall Summary Sheet

Looking at Scores to See Which Children May Need EIR

In general, you are first looking for children for EIR who enter third grade reading on an end-of-grade-1 or grade 2-reading level. If a child falls below 90 percent word-recognition accuracy on a grade 2 passage, she most likely needs supplemental help in word recognition. If a child falls below 65 words correct per minute (wcpm) early in the fall, he probably needs to work on fluency. If a child can tell little about the grade 2 or 3 IRI passage (e.g., gets a score of 1 or 2 on the summarizing rubric) or is at the frustration level (lower than 70 percent correct) on the IRI questions, she most likely needs to work on comprehension.

Providing for Children at Different Reading Levels

EIR lessons are taught to students in a group of no more than seven (which itself is a considerable challenge). If you have room in your group, children who are reading on a third-grade level with a 92 percent to 97 percent accuracy in word recognition but with problems in fluency and/or comprehension could be included. These children may exit the EIR group before the end of the school year, and that is okay. Information to help you decide if children should exit from EIR is provided later in the chapter.

If there are more than seven children in your room who need EIR, I recommend creating two groups instead of just one. If you have a reading resource teacher at your school, perhaps she could take one group and you could take the other. With a situation like this, a number of teachers have reported switching groups periodically so they are in touch with the strengths and weaknesses of all of the EIR students in their classroom.

With two EIR groups, teachers have found that it works best to put the students who are reading at a higher level in one group and the students who are reading at a lower level in the other. In this way, the faster-moving students aren't calling out answers at the expense of the slower-moving students. Also, the slower-moving students will be less inclined to feel discouraged if they do not experience others in their group catching on more quickly.

Sometimes I am asked if a child who is reading on a primer level or lower in the fall of third grade should be placed in the grade 3 EIR group, and my answer is, "No, unfortunately, the EIR grade 3 program, as designed, is too hard for them."

A child who enters third grade reading on a primer level or lower is in need of one-on-one or two-on-one support from a reading specialist. If no other supplemental instruction is available, you could have students join a grade 2 EIR group. However, it is likely that they will only be reading on a second-grade level by the end of the year since the grade 2 EIR lessons are designed to only get a child to a second-grade reading level by May.

Grouping Considerations

The following are grouping considerations that are worth highlighting:

▶ **Keep the group to no more than seven students.** Orchestrate two groups, if need be. Perhaps a reading resource teacher can take one group and you can take the other. Then, you can periodically switch groups so you have a sense of the strengths and weaknesses of all your struggling readers.

▶ **Reserve EIR instruction for teachers only.** Children at risk of reading failure desperately need quality, supplemental reading instruction from a certified teacher. Instructional aides don't have sufficient background.

▶ **Arrange two groups for optimum student participation.** If you have enough students for two groups, put the faster-progressing students in one group and the students who may need more support in the other. In this way, it won't always be the more-advanced students calling out answers at the expense of the slower-progressing students. Also, the slower-progressing students are less inclined to feel discouraged if they do not experience others in their group catching on more quickly.

▶ **Remember, children can exit from an EIR group before the end of the year.** Some students will catch up to their grade-level peers and therefore not need EIR beyond, say, February, sometimes even sooner. Guidelines to help you decide if children are ready to be taken out of EIR are provided later in this chapter.

▶ **ELLs do well in EIR.** Often, I am asked how to handle ELLs and fall placement in EIR. Even if ELLs do relatively poorly on the fall assessment, I would put them in an EIR group in the fall unless they have the opportunity to learn to read in their first language. You do not want to take the chance of preventing any student from learning to read by postponing their participation in EIR to a later time. Also, I have found that ELLs generally do well in EIR (Taylor 2001).

▶ **Special education students do well in EIR.** I have also found EIR works well with students who have learning disabilities. No modifications to the program are recommended.

▶ **The earlier the better.** Do not wait to place a child in EIR even if he or she had low scores on all the assessments. Place them in EIR in the fall if they are reading on an end-of-first-grade level or higher. If you wait to put these students in EIR in January, for example, you are likely ensuring that they will not be reading on a third-grade level by the end of the school year. Students who are reading on a mid-first-grade-level or lower will find the texts in the grade 3 EIR model too difficult and will need a one-on-one or two-on-one intervention to catch on to reading.

Assessing Students' Progress in Reading During the School Year

It is always important to assess students' reading abilities and improvement in order to tailor your instruction. Therefore, opportunities are embedded within the EIR model so that teachers can monitor and document students' progress. Oral reading analysis, oral reading fluency checks, analysis of summaries, and analysis of written answers to questions are four assessments recommended when implementing EIR. (Refer back to Chapter 4 for a discussion about oral reading analysis.)

Assessing Word-Recognition Fluency: Oral Reading Fluency Check

Skilled readers are fluent readers. They are able to read orally with accuracy, automaticity, speed, proper phrasing, and expression. *Automaticity* refers to the ability to recognize words automatically while reading. The benefit of fluent reading is that it enables a reader to devote maximum cognitive capacity to the meaning of text (Kuhn and Stahl 2003; NRP 2000). Less-fluent readers focus their attention on decoding individual words and tend to read in a choppy, word-by-word manner.

One good measure of fluent reading is the number of words read correctly on a grade-level passage in one minute (wcpm score). The number of wcpm has been found to be a useful indicator of a student's reading ability (Fuchs et al. 2001) particularly for students reading on a grade 1–3 level (Kuhn and Stahl 2003). You can have them read passages from the EIR lessons and other texts at their reading level such as those read in guided reading groups. By the end of the school year, you want to see students reading at about 100 wcpm or better.

Hasbrouck and Tindal (2006) published fall, winter, and spring oral reading norms expressed in wcpm for more than 15,000 students in first through fifth grades. The mean scores and standard deviations (in parentheses) are shown in Table 5-1.

Mean Words Correct Per Minute Scores and Standard Deviations

Grade	Mean Fall Score	Mean Winter Score	Mean Spring Score
1		23 (32)	53 (39)
2	51 (37)	72 (41)	89 (42)
3	71 (40)	92 (43)	107 (44)
4	94 (40)	112 (41)	123 (43)
5	110 (45)	127 (44)	139 (45)

Note: Standard deviations appear in parenthesis.

Adapted from Hasbrouck and Tindal (2006).

Table 5-1 Mean Words Correct Per Minute Scores and Standard Deviations

Phrasing and expression while reading are also important aspects of reading fluency. In addition to assessing students' reading fluency through a wcpm score, you can use a rubric to assess student phrasing and expression while reading. The rubric developed by the National Assessment of Educational Practice (NAEP) is presented in Figure 5-4.

Assessing Students' Ability to Summarize Texts in Writing During the Year

Three or four times during the year between the fall and spring assessments, perhaps on Day 5 of the weekly routine, have students write a summary for a reading selection that is several pages long. Use short narrative pieces or short informational texts. Use the four-point narrative summarizing rubric (Figure 5-5) or four-point informational text rubric (Figure 5-6) to score the summary. Share results with individual students and discuss with them ways they can improve their summaries in the future.

NAEP's Oral Reading Fluency Scale

Level 4   Reads primarily in larger, meaningful phrase groups. Although some regressions, repetitions, and deviations from text may be present, these do not appear to detract from the overall structure of the story. Preservation of the author's syntax is consistent. Some or most of the story is read with expressive interpretation.

Level 3   Reads primarily in three- or four-word phrase groups. Some smaller groupings may be present. However, the majority of phrasing seems appropriate and preserves the syntax of the author. Little or no expressive interpretation is present.

Level 2   Reads primarily in two-word phrases with some three-or four-word groupings. Some word-by-word reading may be present. Word groupings may seem awkward and unrelated to larger context of sentence or passage.

Level 1   Reads primarily word by word. Occasional two-word or three-word phrases may occur but these are infrequent and/or they do not preserve meaningful syntax.

From http://nces.ed.gov/pubs95/web/95762.asp, U.S. Department of Education, National Center for Education Statistics

---

Figure 5-4 NAEP's Oral Reading Fluency Scale

Figure 5-5 Narrative Summarizing Rubric

Figure 5-6 Informational Text Summarizing Rubric

Assessing Students' Written Answers to Questions During the Year

Three or four times during the school year, ask students to write answers to eight or ten questions about a text they have read that is at least several pages long. Include high-level thinking questions, and comprehension strategy questions (including vocabulary questions) (Taylor, Garcia, and Pearson 2007). High-level thinking questions ask students to:

▸ Explain or interpret a story event or idea in a nonfiction selection

▸ Provide character interpretation (if text is a narrative)

▸ Discuss a theme or main idea of the selection

▸ Relate to personal experience

Comprehension strategy questions require the use of:

▸ comprehension monitoring

▸ self-questioning

▸ summarizing

▸ using context clues to get at word meanings

Examples of Questions for *Lazy Lion* (Hadithi and Kennaway 1990)

▶ What is the problem in the story? Is it solved? (description of story event)

▶ At the beginning of the story, how does Lion feel about himself? How do you know this? (interpretation of story event)

▶ Why did Lion complain? Was that a good decision? Why or why not? (character interpretation)

▶ How do you think the animals felt after building their houses for Lion? Tell about a time you have felt like this. (character interpretation and relating to students' life)

▶ What did you ask yourself about Lion's actions when you read this story? (strategy: self-questioning)

▶ Look on the last page. What does *wanders* mean? How did you figure it out? (strategy: word meanings through context)

▶ Describe a part of the story that confused you the most. How did you figure it out? (strategy: comprehension monitoring)

▶ What do you think the author's message is in this story? (theme interpretation)

▶ Tell the most important ideas of the story in a few sentences. (strategy: summarizing)

Scoring: Use a three-point rubric to score the students' answers to each question. Select the score from the three-point rubric for each question that best describes the student's answer. Share results with individual students and discuss with them ways they can provide more accurate, complete, and coherent written answers to questions in the future.

RUBRIC FOR AN ANSWER TO A QUESTION

0 Off track

1 On the right track; getting at details; may not be complete

2 Really good; getting at bigger ideas

Examples of Scores for Answers to a Question on *The Lazy Lion*

▶ Why did none of the homes built by the other animals work for the lion? (interpretation of story event)

Answer A: Because he is being mean to them and saying really mean things. Score of 0—Off track

Answer B: He was selfish and mean and didn't think about them and their houses. Score of 1—On the right track

Answer C: They built houses that worked for them and they didn't know how to build a house for a lion. Score of 2—Very good

Scoring Summaries and Answers to Questions as a Group

Teachers have found that they learn a great deal by scoring some of their students' summaries and answers to questions working together (Taylor, Garcia, and Pearson 2007). Here is a process that a group of third-grade teachers used and their comments on the experience.

▶ Randomly select about 10–15 percent of students' summaries and questions.

▶ Identify the types of questions that were asked (e.g., story interpretation/high-level thinking, comprehension strategy, including vocabulary).

▶ Begin reading student responses aloud together and discuss how you would score them and record some of the student responses that fit under scores of 0, 1, or 2 for questions, or 1–4 for summaries, as representative (e.g., anchor) examples of each. As you are scoring, you might update or revise the scoring rubrics.

Teacher Comments

▶ *We didn't think our students would be able to write answers to these questions but we decided to give it a try. We found out they could do it. It changed our perceptions and expectations of what our students can do. We realized we needed to raise the level of our instruction because our kids needed it.*

▶ *By scoring the assessments together we started thinking about how we could improve our instruction. We started talking about asking better questions, prompting students for better responses, and we realized we needed to model high-level response and summarizing.*

▶ *After assessments in November, we all realized that we needed to focus instruction on summarizing. That is one of the major comprehension strategies that our third graders weren't very good at it. We realized that we were asking our kids to summarize but never showed them how to do it. We started talking about how we would model and teach them how to summarize.*

▶ *In the beginning we were excited about the questions we would ask. Then we started to understand that high-level thinking was more than just asking a good question. We had to help students answer the questions and elaborate on their answers.*

▶ *This has been a real revelation because you can use assessment to drive your instruction. It is wonderful when you are actually doing it. We realized we aren't only evaluating what the kids can do; we are also evaluating our thinking and our ideas. Our focus on instruction has become acting as facilitators and doing a lot of modeling and coaching. We have seen the progress our kids are making. And you know, we are raising our expectations for our kids all the time. It has been a really exciting process.*

Taking Children Out of EIR

Often people ask how to determine when children don't need the EIR lessons any longer because they are reading so well. In this section, I list some guideline to help you make this decision. Some children will be ready to leave EIR lessons in January or February, but I have not found this to be too common. In general, I recommend that you be conservative and not take a child out of EIR too quickly.

Criteria for Taking a Child Out of EIR

You may decide it is time for a child to stop coming to EIR lessons because she is reading very well and the EIR lessons seem too easy. The following criteria need to be considered:

▶ The child is able to read grade-level classroom texts cold (e.g., she has not seen or read these texts before) with 95–100 percent accuracy, with good fluency (e.g., at 100 words correct per minute or better), and good comprehension (90 percent correct on questions or a score of 3 or better on the four-point summarizing rubric).

▶ The child has had EIR lessons for at least two months.

▶ The child is clearly ahead of other children when working in a group.

▶ After the child has left the group, watch closely to see if the child is making good progress in the regular program. If not, she may need to rejoin the EIR group.

Spring Assessments

In the spring, you again need to administer an informal reading inventory to evaluate a student's reading (e.g., decoding) level, reading rate (fluency), and comprehension ability. Directions for spring assessments in third grade can be found in Figure 5-7. A summary sheet to record scores is in Figure 5-8 and a summarizing scoring rubric to assess comprehension beyond a students' ability to answer questions is provided in Figure 5–2 on page 70.

Evaluating Students' Progress at the End of the School Year

▶ At the end of the school year, you need to evaluate EIR children's ability to decode a third-grade-level passage with at least 92 percent accuracy. Hopefully, your third-grade children, including ELL students and students with learning disabilities, get to an end-of-third-grade reading level by the end of the year.

▶ I have found that 94 percent of the children who are in a grade 3 EIR group are decoding on at least an end-of-grade-3 level by May (Taylor 2001).

▶ Another factor you have to consider is the child's fluency as measured by words correct per minute. In a national study, Hasbrouck and Tindal (2006) found that the average

Directions for Spring Assessment

Oral reading: Errors include substitutions, omissions, teacher-assisted or teacher-pronounced words. Self-corrections, repetitions, or hesitations are *not* errors.

Step 1. Have student read a Grade 3 passage for 1 minute. Put a check above each word read incorrectly (error). If a student is stuck on a word in this one minute timing give about 5 seconds, then tell the word. Mark the last word read in the minute.

Step 2. Continue reading the passage to the end, marking the errors made. Now that you are no longer timing the student use your own judgment on time before telling a word, but probably give about a five second time wait. Stop if the child is at less than 90 percent word-recognition accuracy on the grade 3 IRI passage (see Step 6), and do not do the summarizing or comprehension questions (continue to Steps 5 and 6).

Step 3. Have student summarize the selection. Use the four point rubric to score (see Summarizing Rubric in Figure 5-2. Record score 1, 2, 3, or 4 on spring summary sheet (see Figure 5-8).

Step 4. Ask student questions for passage. Record the number of questions correct on the questions sheet.

Step 5. Go back and count the number of words read correctly in 1 minute. Record on selection sheet.

Step 6. Go back and count the number of errors in total passage. Calculate word-recognition accuracy. This is the number of words read correctly (total number of words in passage minus error) divided by the total number of words). Record on summary sheet.

If not already done, transfer all information to Spring Summary Sheet.

If student reads the grade 3 passage with 92 percent accuracy or above in word recognition, continue to the grade 4 passage and repeat Steps 1 through 6. Stop if the child is below 90 percent accuracy and do not do the summarizing or comprehension questions on this passage (continue to Steps 5 and 6). However, if the student reads the grade 3 passage with below, but close to, 92 percent accuracy in word recognition, have the student read a second grade 3 passage and repeat Steps 1 through 6. Stop if the child is below 90 percent accuracy and do not do the summarizing or comprehension questions (continue to Steps 5 and 6). If needed because a child was not successful on a grade 3 passage, have him read a grade 2 passage.

Figure 5-7 Directions for Spring Assessment

Grade 3 Spring Summary Sheet

Grade 3	Grade 3 passage from an informal reading inventory					Grade 4 passage from an informal reading inventory				
Student	Words Correct in First Minute	Number of Errors in Total Passage	Word-Recognition Accuracy (Percent Correct)	Summary Score (4-Point Rubric)	Questions Correct (Percent)	Words Correct in First Minute	Number of Errors in Total Passage	Word-Recognition Accuracy (Percent Correct)	Summary Score (4-Point Rubric)	Questions Correct (Percent)

Grade 3	Extra Grade ____ passage from an informal reading inventory					Extra grade ____ passage from an informal reading inventory				
Student	Words Correct in First Minute	Number of Errors in Total Passage	Word-Recognition Accuracy (Percent Correct)	Summary Score (4-Point Rubric)	Questions Correct (Percent)	Words Correct in First Minute	Number of Errors in Total Passage	Word-Recognition Accuracy (Percent Correct)	Summary Score (4-Point Rubric)	Questions Correct (Percent)

Figure 5-8 Spring Summary Sheet

third-grade child was able to read grade 3 passage at the end of the school year with 107 words correct per minute.

▶ You should also be concerned about a child's comprehension as measured by answering passage questions and summarizing. We would like to see a child answer at least 70 percent of the questions correctly and get a summarizing score of 3 or 4. In a national study (Taylor et al. 2000), I found that the average third-grade reader had a retelling score of 3.0.

▶ If a child falls below 92 percent accuracy on the grade 3 passage, he may need supplemental help in word recognition in the fall of fourth grade. If a child falls below 90 wcpm, she may need to work on fluency in the fall. If a child can tell little about the grade 3 passage (score 1 or 2) or is at the frustration level on the questions (falling below 70 percent correct), he may need to work on comprehension in the fall.

Summary

This chapter introduced you to the assessment procedures used to support and successfully implement EIR. Watching students closely as they tackle the complex task of learning to read is imperative so that your teaching can be informed by what students know and are able to do as well as what causes them to struggle. The multiple chances to assess students' reading and comprehension throughout the EIR five-day cycle and transition phase provide you with a framework that offers your struggling readers with the best possible chances for success.

In the next chapter, I take a broader look at the teaching of reading once again so you will be able to dovetail what you've learned about EIR with your regular reading instruction. Specifically, Chapter 6 describes how EIR fits into a reading block and how to provide motivating, intellectually challenging independent learning activities to all of your students while you work with guided reading groups or your EIR group.

Managing Your Reading Block with EIR

I n this chapter, we look at how EIR lessons fit within the reading block, reading/writing block, or literacy block. Teachers arrange their literacy time in ways that suit their individual teaching styles and students' needs, and the EIR lessons are effective in many different iterations of effective instruction. However, as discussed briefly in Chapter 1, some components are in place no matter what: whole-group instruction, small-group instruction (including guided reading and EIR lessons), and independent reading/work for students while the teacher is with small EIR groups.

Take a look at your reading block schedule. Research shows that effective teachers *balance* whole-class and small-group instruction (Pressley et al. 2003; Taylor et al. 2007). My research also shows that too much time on whole-group instruction (e.g., 60 percent or more) or too much time on small group (e.g., 85 percent or more) does not have a positive impact on students' reading growth (Taylor et al. 2000; Taylor et al. 2007).

With this balance in mind, you might begin the reading block with a whole-group lesson in which you provided explicit instruction in a reading skill or strategy, using a high-quality trade book or literature from a basal reader anthology. Teach the reading skill or strategy in the context of students' engaging with and enjoying a story or piece of nonfiction. Then you can move into small guided reading groups to differentiate instruction, including follow-up instruction on the skill or strategy covered in the whole-group lesson. You and your students should be aware of the connections among whole-group, small-group, and one-on-one instruction; it should not be a hidden thread but a visible thread. Students are in a much better position to learn when you explicitly name the connections for them. For example, in Karen Olson's whole-group lesson in Appendix 2-1, she focuses on the reciprocal teaching strategies of predicting, questioning, clarifying, and summarizing with a story on bugs in their *Weekly Reader.* For independent work during small-group time, Karen has students read about other insects in triads and practice the reciprocal teaching strategies they learned. During small guided reading group lessons, Karen again has students work on reciprocal teaching as they read biographies at their reading levels.

Helpful Resources

Fountas, I., and G. S. Pinnell. 1996. *Guided Reading.* Portsmouth, NH: Heinemann..

Lapp, D., D. Fisher, and T. D. Wolsey. 2009. *Literacy Growth for Every Child: Differentiated Small-Group Instruction, K–6.* New York: Guilford.

Manning, M., G. Morrison, and D. Camp. 2009. *Creating the Best Literacy Block Ever.* New York: Scholastic.

Pressley, M. 2006. *Reading Instruction That Works: The Case for Balanced Teaching.* 3d ed. New York: Guilford.

Routman, R. 2003. *Reading Essentials.* Portsmouth, NH: Heinemann.

———. 2008. *Teaching Essentials.* Portsmouth, NH: Heinemann.

Serravallo, J. 2010. *Reading Instruction in Small Groups.* Portsmouth, NH: Heinemann.

Southall, M. 2009. *Differentiated Small-Group Reading Lessons.* New York: Scholastic.

Taberski, S. 2000. *On Solid Ground: Strategies for Teaching Reading K–3.* Portsmouth, NH: Heinemann.

Tyner, B. 2009. *Small-Group Reading Instruction: A Differentiated Teaching Model for Beginning and Struggling Readers.* Newark, DE: International Reading Association.

Tyner, B., and S. E. Green. 2005. *Small-Group Reading Instruction: A Differentiated Teaching Model for Intermediate Grade Readers, Grades 3–8.* Newark, DE: International Reading Association.

Walpole, S., and M. C. McKenna. 2009. *How to Plan Differentiated Reading Instruction: Resources for Grades K–3.* New York: Guilford.

Effective teachers use good classroom management practices (Pressley et al. 2003). There are many excellent professional books, such as those listed in this chapter, that can help you develop and manage a dynamic literacy block, but for now, here are a few key components to implement:

▶ Work with students to establish classroom rules and routines to minimize disruptions and to provide for smooth transitions within and between lessons.

▶ Use positive language and a motivating, engaging environment to impact students' behavior.

▶ Make a conscious effort to develop self-regulated, independent learners.

▶ Create a positive classroom atmosphere by demonstrating enthusiasm for learning, and have high expectations for your students

Management Ideas

Some of the primary-grade teachers I have worked with have engaged in the following practices to promote a constructive, classroom environment. Notice that teachers negotiate the criteria for behavior with students and refine it throughout the year. Some teachers generate and revise lists of expected behaviors and routines as a shared writing activity.

How to Promote Positive Classroom Environments

▶ Generate rules as a class during the first week of school.

▶ Read through classroom rules with students and talk about them at the morning meeting.

▶ Ask students to evaluate their actions after a discussion or activity, focusing on strengths and areas in need of improvement.

▶ Teach students how to compliment each other and encourage them to be respectful of one another.

▶ Have a brief class meeting at the end of the day and ask students how they thought their behaviors were that day, based on the rules they had generated as a class.

▶ Use routines and procedures to handle disruptions effectively and efficiently.

▶ Use routines and procedures to provide for smooth transitions within and between lessons.

▶ Show students that you care about them as individuals, but also let them know that you will be firm, holding them to high standards as learners and good citizens.

▶ Give specific, constructive feedback to students regularly, provide encouragement, and challenge them to think more deeply.

▶ Offer sincere praise to students, as a group or one-on-one, when they have demonstrated behaviors reflected in your classroom rules as well as in school goals defining the school community, often displayed when you enter a building.

Reading Block Schedules: Examples of Effective Balance

The three teachers you met in Chapter 2 typically start their reading block with a 20- to 30-minute whole-group lesson (often broken up with brief partner work) and then move into a few 20- to 30-minute small-group lessons in which they provide differentiated instruction that varies depending on students' reading abilities and needs. All three teachers also provide EIR lessons to their lowest readers. The three teachers explicitly state their lesson purposes in both whole- and small-group lessons. They move at an efficient pace, guided by lesson goals, and meet with as many small groups as possible. Each teacher's schedule is included here along with a brief discussion of how the reading block might be structured.

Karen's Daily Reading Block Schedule

9:00–9:30	Whole-Group Lesson
9:30–9:50	Small-Group 1
9:50–10:10	Small-Group 2
10:10–10:30	Small-Group 3
10:30–10:50	EIR Lesson

Karen has a 110-minute reading block. She spends about 30 minutes a day on a whole-group lesson. She spends about 60 minutes a day on three guided reading groups and 20 minutes on one EIR group (which is a second shot of quality instruction for her struggling readers).

Average and above-average readers spend about 60 minutes a day on three or four independent learning activities that include independent reading and below-average readers spend about 40 minutes a day on independent learning activities. Typically, the below-average readers engage in three independent activities. Sometimes they have follow-up work to complete related to their EIR lesson as one of their three independent activities.

Karen has a parent or senior citizen volunteer in her classroom during her reading block who listens to EIR students reread their EIR stories and provides assistance as students are engaged in independent work activities. This volunteer also goes to the first-grade classroom to support EIR students as they work with their first-grade buddies.

Julie and Lauren also have 100- to 110-minute reading blocks that are similar to Karen's block. Linda works with her EIR group after lunch and the other students complete morning literacy work or engage in independent pleasure reading.

Karen's Typical Daily Reading Block at a Glance

Whole-Group Lesson (30 minutes)	Small-Group Lesson (20 minutes for each group using leveled texts)	EIR Lesson (20 minutes)	Group	Activities for Independent Work Time
Read basal reader selection, target comprehension strategy, teach vocabulary at point of contact, discuss high-level questions, review activities for work time	Coach in word-recognition strategies, as needed, discuss vocabulary at point of contact, provide follow-up to comprehension strategy taught in whole group, discuss high-level questions about leveled text			
X	X		Above-Average Readers*	*Activity 1:* Reading or rereading, writing, discussing as follow-up to whole-group text
				Activity 2: Reading or rereading, writing, discussing as follow-up to small-group text
				Activity 3: Reading or rereading, writing, discussing text unrelated to whole- or small-group lesson
				Activity 4: Reading for pleasure from book of choice
X	X		Average Readers*	Activity 1
				Activity 2
				Activity 3
				Activity 4
X	X		Below-Average Readers**	Activity 1
		X		Activity 2 or 3
				Activity 4

*10–20 minutes for each activity for a total of 60 minutes

**10–20 minutes for each activity for a total of 40 minutes

Independent Activities

A common question that teachers ask as they begin EIR lessons with their struggling readers is, *What are my other students doing when I teach my EIR group?* In order for you to be able to spend quality time with your EIR group, you need to supply independent activities that are challenging and motivating and keep students engaged. Karen, Julie, and Lauren all reported that this was one of their biggest challenges. Therefore, this section includes details about some of the differentiated literacy activities Karen, Julie, and Lauren organized for their students during independent work time as well as some additional suggestions and resources. With these ideas, you should feel energized to not only teach your guided reading groups, but also teach struggling readers in a small-group using EIR intervention strategies, just as Karen, Julie, and Lauren did.

Independent Activities in Karen's, Julie's, and Lauren's Classrooms

Independent activities that Karen, Julie, and Lauren structure for their students include working independently, with a partner, or in a small group on reading, writing in a journal, writing on an open-response sheet, talking with others about what they have read or written about in their reading, and going on the computer to read or gather new information. Below are examples, some of which we read about in Chapter 2. You may be able to use or adapt a number of the open-ended student response sheets in Figures 6-1 to 6-13 (and described later in this chapter) for some of these activities.

See the DVD for full-size versions of all the forms in this chapter.

Practicing and Rating My Reading Fluency

Name _____ Date _____

Title _____

I read my story _____ times.

  a. My reading rate was: Good 😊 Okay 😐 Could Be Better 😞

  b. My phrasing was: Good 😊 Okay 😐 Could Be Better 😞

  c. My expression was: Good 😊 Okay 😐 Could Be Better 😞

I want to work on a, b, or c (circle one).

Figure 6-1 Practicing and Rating My Reading Fluency

Log for Independent Pleasure Reading

Name _____ Date _____

Book Title	Date	Start Page	End Page	My Ideas/Questions Are:

Figure 6-2 Log for Independent Pleasure Reading

Concept Map

Name _____ Date _____

Book Title _____ Page _____

Author _____

It means:		My connection:
	Juicy word:	
Sentence:		An example:

Figure 6-3 Concept Map

Cause-Effect Chart

Name _____ Date _____

Book Title _____

This happened (Cause)	On page	That made this happen (Effect)	On page	My ideas

Figure 6-4 Cause-Effect Chart

Topic Map

Name _____ Date _____

Write words and phrases in the boxes below.

Food:	Habitat:
My animal (topic) is:	Babies:
Appearance:	Interesting facts:

Figure 6-5 Topic Map

Comparison Chart (Example)

Books:

Name:

Date:

	Animal 1: Wolf	Similar (S) or Different (D)	Animal 2: Coyote
Appearance	90 pounds	D	45 pounds
Food	Little animals	S	Little animals
Habitat	Woods	S	Woods
Babies			
Interesting Facts	Travel in a pack	D	Travel alone

Figure 6-6 Example of a Comparison Chart

Fact-Opinion Chart

Name _____

Book Title _____ Author _____

Idea (sentence)	Page	Fact (F) or Opinion (0)	Why?

Figure 6-7 Fact-Opinion Chart

Narrative Summary Sheet

Name _____ Book Title _____

Summarize the story in complete sentences.

Beginning (who, where, problem):	Middle (events):
End (solution):	Author's message:

New Words

Write two words that you did not know or that you found interesting and what you think they mean if you can.

Word	Page	Meaning

Figure 6-8 Narrative Summary Sheet

Summary Sheet for Informational Text

Name _____

Summarize the informational text you read. Write in complete sentences.

PART 1	Main Idea	Important Details
PART 2		
PART 3		

New Words

Write two words and what they mean.

Word	Page	Meaning

Figure 6-9 Summary Sheet for Informational Text

Note-Taking Sheet on Comprehension Monitoring

Name _____ Date _____

Word or idea that confused me	Page	Notes

Figure 6-10 Notes on Comprehension Monitoring

Note-Taking Sheet for Practicing Reciprocal Teaching Strategies

Independent Study Strategy Sheet Using Recriprocal Teaching Model

Name _____ Book Title _____

A. Summarizing the Story

Tell about what you read in one or two sentences (for pages _____).

B. Generating Questions from the Story

Ask two important questions about what you read:

     1. (from page ____)

     2. (from page ____)

C. Clarifying—Check for Understanding

Note other ideas that you have questions about or vocabulary that you need to understand better.

     1. (from page ____)

     2. (from page _____)

D. Predicting

Write a prediction about what you think will be in the next section of the text (if a prediction comes to mind).

Repeat Steps A–D for the next section of the text.

Figure 6-11 *Sheet for Practicing Reciprocal Teaching Strategies*

Note-Taking Sheet for a Book Report

Name _____ Date _____

A. Beginning: Characters, Setting, Problem

B. Events

C. Solution to Problem

D. Author's Message

Share Your Ideas

1. Tell about a part you liked or didn't like, and why.

2. Tell how this is like your life and why.

New Words

Write two words that you did not know or that you found interesting and what you think they mean if you can.

Word	Page	Meaning

Figure 6-12 *Note-Taking Sheet for a Book Report*

Note-Taking Sheet for a Book Club Discussion

Book Title _____

People in my group:

Write two juicy questions about the story (why, how, what do you think?)

1.

2.

Share Your Ideas

1. Tell about a part you liked and why.

2. Tell how this is like your life and why or make a connection to the world around you.

New Words

Write two words and what they mean.

Figure 6-13 *Note-Taking Sheet for a Book Club Discussion*

See the DVD for full-size versions of all the the forms in this chapter.

Complete strategy work as a follow-up to small-group lesson:

- With a partner, finish a topic map on a character from a basal reader story that students started in their whole-class lesson.
- Read and summarize a selected book on a poisonous animal after practicing and summarizing in a whole-group lesson.
- Read and summarize a story at the just-right reading level and generate "big, fat juicy questions" with a partner from the same guided reading group. Be prepared to discuss questions at the next guided reading group lesson.
- Practice reciprocal teaching in triads with books of choice on insects.

▶ **Write in reader response journals and share:**

- Respond to the high-level questions the teacher has written on the board and make text-to-life connections.

▶ **Write on index cards and share:**

- Generate questions, write down interesting or unknown words, write summaries in journals in preparation for book clubs.

▶ **Write on sticky notes and share:**

- Write down the meanings of unknown words from the small-group story.
- Write down a juicy word to share from independent reading.
- Use sticky notes to write down ideas or vocabulary words that need clarifying from texts read, to write phrases to make connections to texts read.

▶ **Read, write, and discuss in book clubs:**

- Read the next chapter or two in a book club book and write good discussion questions/ideas.
- Discuss chapters from a book club book, using questions generated before the club meeting.

▶ **Read, write, and share ideas from informational books:**

- Complete a summary of a section of a National Geographic social studies or science reader at a just-right reading level.
- Write about what was interesting or surprising after reading from a National Geographic social studies or science reader at a just-right reading level.
- Select a planet, do additional reading in books and on the Internet, and write about size, miles from sun and earth, number of moons, and interesting facts to share with whole class after reading about a planet of choice.

▶ **Engage in independent reading for pleasure at just-right (independent) reading level: Keep a log.**

As we can see from the list above, Karen, Julie, and Lauren provide challenging learning activities during independent work time. They have students engage in:

▶ independent and partner work related to high-level talk and writing in response to what they are reading

- student-led discussions of book club books

- researching and writing reports based on books of their own choosing

- independent reading for pleasure from books of their own choosing for about 20 to 30 minutes.

It is important to remember to watch students closely to see if the independent work is both motivating and challenging. Choice is also important. When students are given the opportunity to choose how to respond to the books they've read, they become more engaged in the process and this choice fosters independence and responsibility.

More Suggestions for Challenging Independent Activities

Independent work time can be one of the most academically powerful junctures of the school day, because it's when students actually practice being independent readers. Making independent time work well is crucial because, after all, one of our goals is to create self-regulated and motivated learners.

What factors prevent third graders from learning to read and learning to enjoy reading? Low-level tasks are one major factor. Research by Pressley at al. (2003) has found that teaching behaviors that undermined academic motivation in primary-grade classrooms included tasks with low-task difficulty in which students were asked to complete activities that were too easy, required low cognitive effort, and demanded little of them (80). Students in these classrooms were given activities that were uninspiring, boring, simplistic, and lacked excitement or provided stimulation to students.

In my many visits to third-grade classrooms over the ten years I worked with schools on schoolwide reading improvement (Taylor et al. 2005; Taylor 2010c), I often saw students engaged in primarily low-level tasks during independent work time. Typically, students in these classrooms were reading or rereading basal reader selections or guided reading group books and answering low-level questions, completing worksheets or workbook pages, working on spelling or grammar, and engaging in independent reading with no follow-up or accountability required. Also, these activities often could be completed in much less time than what was allowed, which only compounded the likelihood that students dawdled, got off task, chatted with students near them, or wandered around the room.

At the other end of the spectrum, during my school visits, I also visited exciting classrooms in which students were participating in many tasks requiring high-level thinking and collaboration during independent work time. The levels of student engagement and the numbers of happy faces and excited eyes in these classrooms as compared to classrooms with less motivating activities were striking. Students typically had three or four activities to complete that kept them meaningfully engaged and working at a continuous, efficient pace. With enough to do and with interesting things to work on, they did not get off task. Most important, they appeared to be happy learners.

These observations are supported by research of Pressley and colleagues (2003) on tasks that supported academic motivation in primary-grade classrooms. They found that teachers had motivated learners when they engaged them in cooperative learning and high-order, critical, and creative thinking. For example, in third grade, students might discuss a book in a student-led book club in which high-level questions were written by students on discussion cards before the meeting, or two students might read about, collaboratively write, and co-present a research report on an animal of their own choosing. These teachers also used engaging and interesting texts that aroused students' curiosity, got them excited about their learning, and involved them in excellent literature.

Examples of independent work time activities to engage students and advance their literacy abilities are provided in the next section. Independent student response sheets that go with some of these suggestions are also provided.

Activities That Support Word Recognition and Vocabulary Development

See words for word sorts in *Words Their Way* by Bear, Invernizzi, Templeton, and Johnston (2007).

▶ To reinforce students' knowledge of morphology that you have recently taught in whole group or guided reading groups, have them complete word sorts with a partner. For example, if you have recently focused students' attention on particular roots, prefixes, and suffixes, you could have them sort words containing these roots, prefixes, and suffixes. To practice reading words containing particular morphological elements, students should read the words that have been sorted.

▶ If your school's spelling curriculum uses weekly spelling lists and tests, have students practice spelling misspelled words from their weekly spelling lists after you have given students a pretest and they have self-corrected misspelled words. Word lists should be differentiated based on students' reading and spelling abilities.

For additional suggestions see *Bringing Words to Life: Robust Vocabulary Instruction* by Beck, McKeown, and Kucan (2002).

▶ On sticky notes or in a vocabulary journal, have students write down interesting, unknown, or newly learned words that come from the books they are reading. Students can share words and possible meanings with either the teacher in whole- or small-group lessons or by turning a vocabulary journal in to teacher, or with a volunteer, educational assistant, or older classroom helper.

▶ Have students complete a concept map or web of juicy words identified by their teacher from books they are reading.

Activities That Support Fluency

▶ With a partner, have EIR students reread stories from their guided reading group or EIR lesson. Students should coach one another on difficult words. Refer back to Chapter 3 for prompts students can use during partner reading.

For additional suggestions on fluency, see *The Fluent Reader: Oral Reading Strategies for Building Word Recognition, Fluency, and Comprehension* by Rasinski (2003).

▶ Have EIR students reread stories from their guided reading group or EIR lesson with a volunteer, educational assistant, or older student helper (who coaches as students get stuck on words they cannot decode instantly).

▶ Have students reread stories and informational texts in their book box. They should list books read for fluency and self-rate their fluency on books read. (See Figure 6-1.)

▶ Have students read new books for pleasure. They should log books they read (Figure 6-2).

Activities That Support Comprehension: Skills and Strategies

▶ Have students read books to practice comprehension skills and strategies. Examples of open-ended response sheets include the following: concept map (Figure 6-3), cause-effect chart (Figure 6-4), topic map (Figure 6-5) comparison chart (Figure 6-6), fact/opinion chart (Figure 6-7), summary sheet for narrative text (Figure 6-8), summary sheet for informational text (Figure 6-9), comprehension monitoring sheet (Figure 6-10), reciprocal teaching sheet (Figure 6-11).

▶ Have students write questions as they read or after they are finished reading. Question types include: clarifying, main idea, summary, interpretive, evaluative/critical literacy.

Activities That Support Comprehension: Learning New Information

Have students engage in the following:

▶ Read books to learn new information about topics of interest.

▶ Search and read on the internet to learn more information.

▶ Read books, magazines, and other texts that address social studies and science curriculum. Teachers, the media specialist, or volunteers could locate existing books at the school or purchase books (with school funds, funds from PTA or local businesses) at various reading levels that cover topics in social studies and science curriculum for grade 3.

▶ Prepare and give an oral or written presentation with a partner, triad, or independently. (See Figure 6-12.)

▶ Prepare a written report. Students could do reports with a partner, triad, or independently. (See Figure 6-5 as a way to organize ideas.) Other types of writing after reading include: procedures, recounting an event, explanation, interpretation, and persuasion.

▶ From independent reading on topics of interest, write down words to share (vocabulary) and write about them (Figure 6-3).

Activities That Support Comprehension: Talk and Writing About Text

After the teacher has modeled and done coaching lessons, students can:

▶ Participate in literature circles: learn routines, read, take notes, and share (Figure 6-13).

▶ Respond to literature (Figure 6-12, 6-13).

▶ Prepare and give a book report (Figure 6-12).

▶ Engage in critical literacy, in which students evaluate, express, discuss, and/or write ideas related to an issue they have read about (Heffernan 2004).

For more suggestions, see
Comprehension Shouldn't Be Silent by Kelley and Clausen-Grace (2007).
Reciprocal Teaching at Work: Strategies for Improving Reading Comprehension by Oczkus (2003).
QAR Now by Raphael, Highfield, and Au (2006).

For more suggestions, see
Reading and Writing Informational Text in the Primary Grades by Duke and Bennett-Armistead (2003).
Informational Text in K–3 Classrooms: Helping Children Read and Write by Kletsien and Dreher (2005).

For more suggestions see
Book Club: A Literature-Based Curriculum, 2d ed., by Raphael, Pardo, and Highfield (2002).
Moving Forward with Literature Circles by Day, Speigel, McLellan, and Brown (2002).
Critical Literacy and Writer's Workshop: Bringing Purpose and Passion to Student Writing by Heffernan (2004).
Using Literature to Enhance Content Area Instruction: A Guide for K–5 Teachers by Olness (2007).

What Should I Read Aloud? by Anderson (2007).

Literature and the Child 7th ed., by Galda, Cullinan, and Sipe (2010).

Activities That Support Reading for Pleasure

Have students:

▶ Read books from different genre for 20 to 30 minutes a day. After reading, have students complete a reading log (Figure 6-2).

▶ Read different books from a favorite author.

▶ Share favorite books in a book sharing club.

▶ Write about favorite books on cards for a book file that other students can look through for book suggestions.

Independent work time is an important component of a teacher's overall classroom reading program. Students spend a considerable amount of time working on their own or with others while teachers work with small, guided reading groups. It is crucial that students are actively engaged in interesting, challenging learning activities that meet their needs and move them forward in literacy abilities during this independent work time. However, it is easy for these independent learning activities to become routine, undifferentiated, unnecessary practice, and not motivating or challenging to students. When this happens, it is easy for students to get off task or to spend much more time that is needed on assigned activities. To alleviate these issues, many teachers find that changing the independent activities every so often works well, as does providing students with choice. Additionally, providing students with long-term projects (e.g., author studies, research projects) can also avert some of the routinization of the activities. Never underestimate the power of sharing ideas with colleagues about effective independent learning activities.

For more on effective, motivating reading instruction and assessment in general:

Classroom Reading Assessment: Making Sense of What Students Know and Do by Paratore and McCormick (2007).

Reading Instruction That Works: The Case for Balanced Teaching, 3d ed., by Pressley (2006).

On Solid Ground: Strategies for Teaching Reading K–3 by Taberski (2000).

For more on differentiated reading instruction:

Differentiated Small-Group Reading Lessons by Southall (2009).

How to Plan Differentiated Reading Instruction: Resources for Grades K–3 by Walpole and McKenna (2009).

Differentiated Instruction in Reading by Robb (2007).

Creating an EIR Community

Early Intervention in Reading is a powerful approach for accelerating the reading development of children who find learning to read difficult, and in some respects it's easy to implement. The predictable structure, the small-group attention, the motivating literature at its heart make it something that teachers and children quickly grow to like. However, because it isn't a curriculum but rather a repertoire of teaching strategies, and because any learner who struggles requires teachers to reflect and use considerable skill, I strongly encourage teachers to enlist support along the following three lines:

1. Teachers need to work with colleagues during their first year of teaching EIR lessons.

First and foremost, over many years, I have found that teachers experience more success with their students when they regularly participate in monthly meetings with colleagues to discuss EIR during the first year they are teaching the lessons. Together, teachers can clarify procedures, share successes, and help one another solve problems. Taking on EIR and weaving it in to effective whole-group and small-group instruction amounts to highly differentiated teaching—not an easy thing to achieve.

In a research study on effective reading practices (Taylor et al. 2000), the most effective schools had a collaborative model for delivering reading instruction in which struggling readers received a second, 30-minute small-group reading

intervention each day to accelerate their literacy learning. Therefore, I strongly recommend that classroom teachers, Title 1 and other reading resource teachers, ELL teachers, and special education teachers who teach together meet as a group in monthly EIR professional learning experiences. Also, I want to stress that classroom teachers can provide the EIR instruction, or at least share the teaching of EIR lessons if they are working with a resource teacher. I developed this model with classroom teachers in mind—in other words, with the notion that classroom teachers can learn to provide extra help to students who need more reading support them during the literacy block.

2. Teachers need to get help from others on scheduling the monthly meetings and sustaining the one-on-one coaching conferences that are an essential piece of EIR.

If numerous teachers are learning about and teaching EIR in the same year, it is extremely helpful if a school has a building facilitator to provide support. This person can take responsibility for securing EIR books and materials, for scheduling of professional learning sessions, for establishing the one-on-one coaching component of EIR by aides, volunteers, or older students (as discussed briefly in Chapter 4 and later in this chapter); and for problem-solving as issues arise.

3. Teachers need to do outreach to parents/caregivers, so that they can help their children practice reading at home.

Parents have a critical role to play in EIR. Children take their EIR story home at the end of the third day so they can read to their parents and get ready for their cross-age tutoring with a first-grade student, or EIR partner, as described in Chapter 3. In Figure 7-1, there is an Individual Take-Home sheet for parents to sign. In Figure 7-2, coaching prompts are provided for parents so that when they are listening to their children read they can help if the child gets stuck on a word as they are reading. Parents should sign the EIR take-home sheets and have their children bring them back to school.

To introduce EIR activities to parents, a sample letter you can send home explaining the program is shown in Figure 7-3. Also, at the beginning of the school year, you can invite parents and students to an "EIR Party," perhaps at the school's back-to-school-night event, in which you explain the materials that will be coming home and the importance of parents'/caregivers' involvement in these activities. You can demonstrate the coaching prompts for parents at this time. Also, you may want to show parents a video of yourself coaching children in their EIR group. Children can come along to the party and eat cookies to make it seem like a festive event.

For parents who can't make it to school, you can send home a video of yourself reading with their child and coaching as the child is stuck on difficult words. One teacher reported taping each child in November and May and then giving the tape to the parents at the end of the year. Another strategy teachers have used for involving parents is inviting them to school to see EIR lessons in action.

Individual Take-Home Sheet

Book Title _____

Name _____ **Date** _____

Parent or Guardian Signature _____

Reading for Fluency

I practiced my story _____ times.

_____ I am ready to read it to my first grader (or EIR partner).

_____ I need to practice some more.

Discussion

Write down one question so you and your first grader (or EIR partner) can talk about the story.

New Words

Write down two words to ask or tell your first grader (or EIR partner) about what they mean.

Figure 7-1 Individual Take-Home Sheet

Coaching Tips for Reading with Third-Grade Readers at Home

In EIR, teachers help children learn to depend on themselves to figure out hard words. To work on this at home, try one of the following prompts or tips when a child gets stuck or makes a mistake:

1. Wait and see if they work it out.

2. Say, "Try that again."

3. Say, "Break the word into chunks and sound it out."

4. Say, "Think about what would make sense."

If the word is a hard one, you may want to tell the child the word. But if the word is an easy one, try one or more of these tips listed before you give the child the word.

Figure 7-2 Coaching Tips for Reading with Third-Grade Readers at Home

Parent/Guardian Information Letter

Dear Parent/Guardian,

To help maximize your child's success in reading, we are using supplementary reading lessons called Early Intervention in Reading (EIR). EIR will help your child by using a different approach to experience reading success. We are excited about it!

We want to emphasize that we really need your involvement. How can you help? Watch for a book and/or take-home activities your child will bring home. Be sure to listen to your child read the story and help with the take-home activities. Return the take-home activity with your signature. Research shows, *"Kids who read the most, read the best!"*

This is the way we teach EIR:

▶ The teacher guides students to use reading strategies as they read a story at their reading level in the small group or with partners.

▶ The teacher and students talk about the story, learn new words, and prepare to read and teach their story to a first-grade student or EIR partner. Children write about the story, based on activities the teacher has provided.

▶ The children practice reading the book at home, and come up with a good question to ask their first-grade buddy or EIR partner and two vocabulary words to teach to their first grader or discuss with their EIR partner whom they will work with one day a week. If they are working with a younger children, they will also listen to this child read and coach them as they get stuck on words in their first-grade stories.

Remember: Listen to your child read the book and assist with the take-home activities. Your child will return the completed take-home activities page with your signature.

Thank you for your continued support as we work together to help your child have success in reading.

Sincerely,

Figure 7-3 Parent/Guardian Information Letter

*See the DVD for full-size
versions of all the the forms
in this chapter.*

Overview of Monthly EIR Meetings

Now let's look at a yearly framework for professional learning sessions that includes how often to have meetings, sample agendas, and suggestions for what to address throughout the year.

At monthly meetings of about an hour, teachers learning to teach EIR lessons can work together to gain expertise and confidence about doing these intervention lessons, hone their abilities to coach children to use word-recognition strategies, depend on themselves, and pose questions about the EIR stories that lead to high-level, comprehension-building responses. Swapping successes, trials, classroom management ideas, and authentic independent activities—teachers can support one another around so many teaching issues.

Begin the meetings in August or September and continue through May. If it's hard to find an hour once a month, you can meet for shorter times over several days during the month. In the first 10 to 15 minutes, the group can focus on sharing ideas and concerns related to EIR lessons. Teachers can also take about 30 to 40 minutes to review and discuss grade-level procedures and the videos clips of effective practice found on the DVD. By November, I encourage teachers to bring their own video segments of teaching EIR lessons.

August

In August, read and discuss Chapters 1 and 2 with the group of teachers in your school who are participating in the EIR professional learning sessions. You may also want to read and discuss Chapter 6, which covers fitting EIR into your daily literacy block and making sure your independent work activities are challenging, motivating, and engaging so you can focus your attention on the students in your guided reading groups or EIR lessons.

September

Additionally, in August or early September, you should begin to review the EIR procedures in Chapter 3. During the September and October meetings, go through the five-day EIR routines for the first time in detail. Also, during monthly meetings, you can revisit certain aspects of the EIR procedures as questions arise.

October

Sometimes teachers report uneasiness about "doing the EIR procedures correctly" and want to delay getting started. However, I always tell teachers not to worry if they are doing things "just right" at first; they will get better at using EIR strategies over time. What is important is to get started with EIR lessons as close to October 1 as possible. Most children who will benefit from EIR need the intervention all year. Students should have the opportunity to be a part of reading intervention lessons that make them feel successful as soon as possible before feelings of discouragement about reading set in.

Monthly Meeting Overview

August/September	Discuss Chapters 1, 2, and 3 Watch videos Review fall assessments Prepare for October meeting
October	Status report on EIR teaching and review procedures as questions arise Review video-sharing procedures Discuss one-on-one coaching Prepare for November meeting
November	Status report on EIR teaching and review of daily procedures Status report of one-on-one coaching Video viewing/sharing Prepare for December meeting
December	Status report on EIR teaching and one-on-one coaching Coaching for comprehension Group activity: Book lesson share Grade-level procedures: Working with informational books Video sharing Prepare for January meeting
January	Status report on EIR teaching Coaching for comprehension Grade-level procedures: Oral reading analysis Video viewing/sharing Prepare for February meeting
February	Status of children's progress Grade-level procedures: Reflections on helping students write answers to questions Group activity: Discuss oral reading analysis Video sharing Prepare for March meeting
March	Status of children's progress Discuss teaching comprehension strategies to enhance students' understanding of informational text Video sharing Prepare for April meeting
April	Status of children's progress Review spring assessment procedures Discuss EIR plans for next year
May (if time permits, or at a grade-level meeting)	Discuss results of assessments Status of children's progress Continue to discuss EIR plans for next year

Table 7-1 Monthly Meeting Overview

November–May

Beginning in November, I recommend you incorporate video sharing into your monthly EIR meetings. To do this, teachers take turns bringing in a 5- to 8-minute video clip of their EIR teaching to share and discuss. These video-sharing experiences give teachers the opportunity to reflect on and discuss their practice. So often, professional development focuses on curriculum lessons tied to a teacher's manual or the proper use of new materials. Teachers are rarely given the opportunity, with the help of colleagues, to think, talk about, and enhance their own teaching practices.

The focus of the video sharing should be:

▶ What the children are doing well or the strengths they are demonstrating in the EIR lesson

▶ What the teacher is doing well to foster strategy use, independence, and success in the children

▶ What else the teacher might have done to foster strategy use, independence, and success.

Through EIR ongoing professional learning sessions, you will improve your coaching abilities. As you focus on coaching and work at it collaboratively, you are reminded that coaching children to become independent is not easy. However, you also learn that coaching is something you can master, with the end result of having more children in your classrooms reading well by the end of the school year. Video-sharing procedures are described in greater detail in Figure 7-4.

Recommended agendas for the year are detailed on the following pages. I suggest you read through them now as a way to get an idea of what a year of EIR professional learning might look like. Then, use the monthly agenda pages to organize and forward your EIR work and learning.

Agendas for Monthly Meetings

In the following section, a yearly framework for monthly meetings, including aspects of the EIR you might focus on during certain months, a structure for sharing and discussing progress and concerns, as well as protocols for viewing and sharing videos is presented.

September Meeting (70–75 min.)

Recommended activities for professional learning in September include the following:

Review Chapters 1, 2, and 3 (10–15 min.)

First, in September, talk about any remaining questions or issues you have related to Chapters 1 and 2. You may also wish to discuss Chapter 6, which covers fitting EIR into your daily schedule and offers ideas for productive independent work for other students while you are working with you EIR group.

Discuss Instructional Procedures in Chapter 3 (35–40 min.)

Carefully work through Chapter 3 and the grade 3 EIR routines. Also, watch the related video clips on the DVD.

Review Assessment Procedures in Chapter 5 (20 min.)

Review the fall assessment procedures described in Chapter 5. Select passages from an informal reading inventory that you will all use in the fall assessments to determine which students need EIR lessons.

Prepare for October Meeting (5 min.)

Briefly review what needs to be done before the October meeting:

▶ You should have your EIR children identified. Don't worry if you aren't quite sure about your placement decisions. You can ask questions in October and make changes then.

▶ You should start your EIR lessons before you meet in October and as close to October 1 as possible. You will get a lot more out of the October meeting if you have already started to teach EIR lessons. You should jot down notes on this instruction so you have a chance to share experiences and to get questions answered at the October meeting.

Often, teachers say they aren't ready to get started yet, but I tell them to simply "take the plunge" and realize that you will be getting better at teaching EIR lessons as the year moves along. The best way to learn about EIR instructional strategies is to start teaching EIR lessons. Good luck!

October Meeting (65–70 min.)

This month you will continue to learn and talk about procedures in grade-level groups. Additionally, you need to prepare for video sharing, which should begin in November. You also need to make sure the one-on-one reading coaching will be in place soon if it's not already.

Status Report on EIR Teaching (10 min.)

Take turns reporting on how things have gone so far with the initial teaching of EIR lessons.

Review Video-Sharing Procedures (20 min.)

Each person should bring one video to share in November, December, or January and a second in February, March, or April. Share one or two videos each month. To learn about video sharing, see Figure 7-4.

The basic approach to video sharing was developed for the EIR Professional Development Program but has also been used in other teacher professional development venues. Each video-sharing segment should take no more than 15 minutes. Focus on students' strategy use, independence, and success.

Prior to coming to your study group, do the following:

1. Videotape the lesson segment you selected. It should be about 5 minutes long.

2. Answer the following three video-sharing questions based on your video:

   ▶ What were things the children were able to do related to your focus area? What things were going well?

   ▶ What was the teacher doing to help children develop and be successful related to your focus area?

   ▶ What else could have been done to foster development and success related to your focus area?

When you share the video at an EIR session, do the following:

1. Share 1 minute of background about the lesson.

2. Tell the group something you would like their help with.

3. View the video with the group.

4. Break into groups of three to review the three video-sharing questions. Take notes on things the children did well, things the teacher in the clip did well in getting children to develop and succeed related to the focus area, and suggestions for things that might have been done differently to help the children develop and success related to the focus area.

5. Discuss the video clip as a larger group. (View the video again if group feels it need to.) The facilitator will ask the three video-sharing questions to the group. Members from the groups of three can share points that they wish to share. Notes from small groups should be given to the teacher who brought the video clip of her teaching.

6. The teacher who brought the clip should ask for their help with item 2.

Remember, this is first and foremost a learning activity in which colleagues are helping one another improve their abilities as coaches.

At an EIR session, sign up for a topic—one part of one day's lesson.

People should sign up for the video sharing in October (see Figure 7-5). If you have more than six teachers in your group, break into groups of from three to five members for the video sharing part of the meeting. With six members in a video-sharing group, you would watch two videos a month. With three members in a video-sharing group, you would watch one video a month. Everyone should share their first video in November, December, or January, and a second video in February, March, or April.

Engaging in Video Sharing

The basic approach to video sharing was developed for the EIR Professional Development Program but has also been used in other teacher professional development venues. Each video-sharing segment should take no more than 15 minutes. Focus on students' strategy use, independence, and success.

Prior to coming to your study group, do the following:

a. Videotape the lesson segment you selected. It should be about 5 minutes long.

b. Answer the following three video-sharing questions based on your video:

  ▶ What were things the children were able to do related to your focus area? What things were going well?
  ▶ What was the teacher doing to help children develop and be successful related to your focus area?
  ▶ What else could have been done to foster development and success related to your focus area?

When you share the video at an EIR session, do the following:

1. Share 1 minute of background about the lesson.

2. Tell the group something you would like their help with.

3. View the video with the group.

4. Break into groups of three to review the three video-sharing questions. Take notes on things the children did well, things the teacher in the clip did well in getting children to develop and experience success related to the focus area, and offer suggestions for things that might have been done differently to help the children develop and experience success related to the focus area.

5. Discuss the video clip as a larger group. (View the video again if group feels it needs to.) The facilitator will ask the three video-sharing questions to the group. Members from the groups of three can share points that they wish to share. Notes from small groups should be given to the teacher who brought the video clip of her teaching.

6. The teacher who brought the clip should ask for their ideas related to with item 2.

Remember, this is first and foremost a learning activity in which colleagues are helping one another improve their skills as coaches. At an EIR session, sign up for a topic—one part of one day's lesson.

Figure 7-4 Engaging in Video Sharing

Video Sharing—Sign-Up Sheet for Grade 3

Month	Teacher	Description of Video
November		Teacher models and coaches on decoding strategies for multisyllabic words as students read book on Day 1
		Coaching for comprehension
		Use of group sheet for narrative
December		Use of individual take-home sheet
		Teacher coaches as children read story on Day 2 or Day 3
		Cross-age tutoring session
January		Use of question sheet on informational book
		Debriefing on Day 5
		Coaching for comprehension
February		Teacher coaches as children read story on Day 2 or 3
		Cross-age tutoring session
		Use of question sheet on informational book
March		Coaching for comprehension, or comprehension monitoring, or reciprocal teaching
		Working with students on grade-level text (word recognition, vocabulary, comprehension)
		Debriefing on Day 5
April		Coaching for comprehension, or summarizing, or reciprocal teaching
		Working with students on grade-level text (word recognition, vocabulary, comprehension)
		Topic to be decided, based on group's need

Figure 7-5 Video Sharing—Sign-Up Sheet for Grade 3

One-on-One Coaching (10 min.)

Discuss the status of the one-on-one coaching piece of EIR or the plans for getting this component in place as soon as possible. Remember, this piece is only needed for those students in your group who are having difficulties with decoding. One-on-one coaches might be educational assistants, classroom volunteers, or older students who are classroom helpers who receive training on how to be a coach. (See the section on training coaches later in this chapter.)

To get maximum results with EIR for students who need additional support in word recognition, one-on-one coaching needs to occur on a regular basis. Children need the opportunity to practice reading with no other child next to them calling out a word they don't know. Also, individual children need the chance to show themselves what they are able to do on their own. Even if you are not responsible for training the one-on-one coaches, you should look through the information presented on this topic in this chapter so you understand the training the coaches have received. Also, as the classroom teacher, you need to supervise the one-on-one coaches and give constructive feedback as needed.

Review of EIR Procedures (20-25 min.)

Refer to your notes about your EIR lessons and raise any questions you have; other members in your group may have the answers. You may want to return to the section in Chapter 3 on grade-level routines to answer questions.

You may find it helpful to consider the following observations I have about EIR lessons and students in October.

- In the fall of third grade, many of the children in EIR still need to work on their reading fluency. They can decode, but they are very slow. They also need to develop confidence in how to attack multisyllabic words. Review the strategy for attacking multisyllabic words in Chapter 3. This needs to be tied to the use of the advanced vowel chart. I also find it helpful to keep stressing that this strategy will only get kids close to the real word. They need to be thinking of a word that will make sense in the story as they are trying to sound out a word. Review and discuss Videos 1 and 2.

- As children get ready to tutor, you need to discuss strategies with them for working with their younger student. They need to understand how to coach, not tell their younger child a word. At the same time, many of them often come up with strategies that are too advanced, such as the multisyllabic strategy they are working on for themselves. Refer back to Figure 3-8 for prompts they can use for partner reading. Also, be sure to have the third-grade children practice the grade 1 story before they work with their first-grade student. I often find they have trouble reading the grade 1 story without practicing it first. Review and discuss Videos 7 and 8.

Preparation for November meeting (5 min.)

For the November meeting, one or two people should bring in short video clips to share predetermined segments of EIR lessons. (See sign-up sheet in Figure 7-5.) An example of a segment would be Steps 1, 2, or 3, or 4 from Days 1, 2, or 3.

November Meeting (60–75 min.)

Status Report on EIR Teaching (10 min.)

Share successes and continued questions you have about EIR teaching.

One-on-One Coaching, Status Report (5 min.)

Discuss how this is working for students who need coaching. Discuss any scheduling issues or concerns.

Questions About the Video Sharing (5 min.)

Discuss any questions or concerns about video sharing, logistics, and feelings you may have had about the video taping.

Discussion of Grade-Level Procedures (20 min.)

▶ By now you are probably feeling more comfortable with the EIR routine. However, in November it is important to consider your timing in EIR lessons. You want to be sure you are getting to all of the parts of a lesson. Discuss strategies for getting through all parts of a lesson.

▶ If there are parts of the EIR routine that you want to review, return to the relevant sections of Chapter 3 and the corresponding video clips.

▶ It is important to remember to have a debriefing session for your children after they work with their younger student. Begin with sharing things that went well and then turn to problems that need to be solved. Discuss what topics are being raised by students in these sessions.

▶ Discuss the activities you have tried for Step 2 of Day 5 (or for Days 4 and 5 if your students are not engaged in cross-age tutoring). Remember, choices include having students bring their basal reader or social studies book to EIR so you can work on attacking multisyllabic words, vocabulary, and comprehension; letting children read independently from books of their own choosing while you coach on word recognition and comprehension or conduct an oral reading analysis or oral reading fluency check; having students write summaries or answers to text so you can assess their abilities and growth on these comprehension tasks.

Video Sharing (15–30 min.)

Share one or two videos, depending on the size of your group.

Preparation for December Meeting (5 min.)

For the December meeting, one or two people (depending on the size of your group) should bring in short video clips to share predetermined segments of EIR lessons.

☑ **tips**

Many teachers are nervous about the video sharing, but they also find that it gets a lot easier by the second time around. In May, on EIR evaluations, many teachers state that the video sharing was one of the most valuable parts of EIR professional learning sessions. So hang in there with the video-sharing experience.

December Meeting (65–80 min.)

Status Report on EIR Teaching (10 min.)

By December, the EIR procedure should seem like second nature. Therefore, it is a good time to reflect on your coaching for comprehension. Keep a list of the questions you ask your students, jot down notes on your questioning practices, and bring them to share at January meeting.

The following are some questions to get you thinking about your questioning and coaching for comprehension.

▶ Are you asking follow-up questions to get a child to clarify what they are saying or to elaborate on their ideas?

▶ Are you giving a child enough wait time?

▶ Are you coaching quiet children (e.g., those who like to say, "I don't know") to talk instead of just moving on to another child?

▶ Are you asking questions that are based on a concept in the story but that leave the story behind and instead relate to children's lives? (For example, after reading *Gila Monsters Meet You at the Airport* [Sharmat 1990], ask, "Think about a time that you had and idea, or impression about someplace or someone that turned out to be untrue. Jot down just a little that tells about this time. Share with your neighbor.")

▶ Are your questions thought provoking and meaningful to the children? (For example, after reading "The Old Mouse" in *Mouse Tales* [Lobel 1972] in which some little mice help an old mouse even though he has been unkind to them, ask "Think about a time you helped someone you did not know very well. What did you do? Why did you do this? Jot down your ideas and tell a partner." Let one person share. Why is this question more thought provoking than asking, "Tell about an older person you have met"?)

One-on-One Coaching, Status Report (5 min.)

It is very important that this component of EIR be up and running for those students who need additional support in word recognition. If possible, try to observe your one-on-one coaches so you can give them feedback.

Group Activity (10 min.)

Using the books you will be using in future EIR lessons, with a partner, generate good coaching for comprehension questions. Share these with the larger group.

Grade-Level Procedures (15 min.)

▶ Remind the children of the purpose of summarizing stories. This is something they may need to do when they are telling their parents or a friend about a book or story they have read. The person they are talking to won't want to hear every detail about the story, so they need to be able to tell about it in just a few sentences.

▶ By now you should be starting to use some of the informational books if you haven't already done so. The written questions are supposed to to get children to read questions correctly, understand the questions, and answer all parts of written questions. Another purpose is to get children to answer in complete sentences. A third purpose is to help them learn how to get their thoughts down on paper in a clear yet concise manner. Sometimes children's written answers are either too general or too long and involved. As you move to the harder informational books, the questions should get more complex in terms of asking the children to summarize the most important ideas or getting them to explain processes or concepts they have read about.

Video Sharing (15–30 min.)

Engage in video sharing.

Preparation for January Meeting (2 min.)

For the January meeting, two people per small group should bring in short video clips to share a predetermined piece of an EIR lesson. Remember to bring in the notes from your coaching for comprehension.

January Meeting (70–75 min.)

Status Report on EIR Teaching (5–10 min.)

Briefly report on successes you are seeing with your students—even after the holiday break!

Coaching for Comprehension (10 min.)

At the December meeting, questions were presented to help you focus on your questioning and coaching for comprehension. Discuss your notes and anything you learned about your practice from focusing on these questions.

▶ Are you asking follow-up questions to get a child to clarify what they are saying or to elaborate on their ideas?

▶ Are you giving a child enough wait time?

▶ Are you working with quiet children who likes to say, "I don't know," instead of just moving on to another child?

▶ Are you asking questions that are based on a concept in the story or informational piece but that leave the story behind and relate to children's lives?

▶ Are your questions thought provoking and meaningful to the children?

On-on-One Coaching, Status Report (5 min.)

In December, you should have found the time to observe your one-on-one coaches and give them feedback. Discuss issues and concerns.

Grade-Level Procedures (20 min.)

If you have students who are still struggling with word recognition, begin oral reading analysis with them (Taylor et al. 1995), perhaps on Day 3 or 5, if you have not already done so. In oral reading analysis, you take three, 100-word samples of a student's reading of material not read before at their instructional level (92–97 percent to determine one problem area to focus on. You provide instruction in this focus area. As a student does subsequent oral readings, you continue to assess in this focus area, monitoring with a progress chart to document the student's growth in the target area. Once a student has made good progress in one problem area, move to another as needed. Oral reading analysis is discussed in greater detail in Chapter 4.

Small-Group Activity. Discuss oral reading analysis as described in Chapter 4. Try oral reading analysis with at least one student over the next month and be prepared to share results at the next month's meeting.

Video Sharing (15 min.)

Engage in video sharing. Fill out a new video-sharing sheet for February through April (refer back to Figure 7-5).

Preparation for February Meeting (5 min.)

For the February meeting, two people per small group should bring in short video clips to share a predetermined piece of an EIR lesson.

February Meeting (60–80 min.)

Status Report on Children's Progress (5–10 min.)

Briefly report on successes you are seeing with your students.

Discuss Grade-Level Procedures (15 min.)

▶ Discuss the successes and challenges you are experiencing with helping students write answers to questions for informational books. Brainstorm solutions to problems.

▶ Discuss successes and challenges you are experiencing with the cross-age tutoring component. Brainstorm solutions to problems.

Group Activity (10 min.)

Those of you who have tried oral reading analysis with students should share your experiences. Help answer one another's questions. When are you doing this? What passages are you using? Discuss challenges. Brainstorm solutions to challenges.

Video Sharing (15–30 min.)

Engage in video sharing.

Preparation for March Meeting (2 min.)

Read about instruction in reciprocal teaching, summarizing, and comprehension monitoring with informational text in Chapter 4. Be ready to talk about this at the next meeting.

Two people should bring in short video clips of their EIR lesson to share.

March Meeting (50–75 min.)

Status Report on Children's Progress (5–10 min.)

Briefly report on successes you are seeing with your students. Also discuss any concerns you may have.

Grade-Level Procedures (20–25 min.)

Teaching Reciprocal Teaching Strategies for Comprehension of Informational Text

If you feel your students are ready for a new challenge, you may wish to try the reciprocal teaching model with them for the last few months of school. In this model, children work in a group as they go through the steps of asking important questions, summarizing, clarifying confusions, and predicting as a way to study-read informational texts, including textbooks they will be asked to read in social studies and science. To learn about implementing reciprocal teaching, see Chapter 4.

If you feel the use of the reciprocal teaching model would be too advanced for your students, I recommend that you still focus during the last few months of school on children's reading and comprehension of informational books. Without using the complete reciprocal teaching model, you may wish to help children work on summarizing the key ideas of a page or so of text in only two to three sentences and/or understanding the concept of comprehension monitoring (i.e., that what they read has to make sense, or they should go back and try a fix-up strategy). To work on summarizing or comprehension monitoring one at a time, see Chapter 4.

Small-Group Activity. Discuss your plans for working with your students on comprehension of informational text. Also, briefly discuss children's progress in word recognition through use of oral reading analysis.

Video Sharing (15–30 min.)

Engage in video sharing.

Preparation for the April Meeting (5 min.)

Before the next meeting, read through the section in Chapter 5 on spring assessments. At the April meeting, you should review spring assessment procedures and answer any questions members of the group may have.

April Meeting (50–65 min.)

Status Report on Children's Progress (5–10 min.)

Briefly report on successes you are seeing with your students.

Assessments (25–30 min.)

Review the steps for completing the assessments in Chapter 5. Select the passages you will all use from an informal reading inventory. Typically, you should do the assessments during the first two weeks of May before things get really wild at the end of the school year.

Preparation for May Meeting

Be prepared to discuss your assessments and your overall reflections about the year, plus plans for next year.

May Meeting (50-65 min.)

Status of Children's Progress

Share your major successes. How many students will be discontinued? How many will require EIR next year?

Discuss Results of Assessments

Discuss how students did on the assessment and which assessments provided you with the most information. Were there any surprises (e.g., did some students whom you thought would do well not do well? Did some students do much better than you expected?)?

Review Year and Discuss Plans for Next Year

Training One-on-One Coaches

The one-on-one coaching component of EIR for students who need more support in word recognition is a very important piece, but one that sometimes gets overlooked simply because it can be difficult to put in place if people are not readily available to read with students every day. However, the students who are having difficulties with word recognition make much better progress in reading if they have a chance every day, or as close to every day as possible, to practice reading their newest EIR story with a person who has been trained in how to coach, not tell them words, as they get stuck. Also, in this one-on-one situation, children get to demonstrate to themselves their decoding abilities and don't have the pressure of another child sitting next to them calling out a word before they do.

Ceilia Huxley, an EIR trainer, developed the material in this section to train coaches. She has used it successfully with instructional aides and parent volunteers.

Coaching Training in One-on-One Coaching

Follow the agenda in Figure 7-6 to provide training to volunteers, educational assistants, and older students who will be coaching EIR students as they read their EIR stories in a one-on-one situation. To introduce EIR, first review the basic elements of the program (Figure 7-7).

Coaching Training Agenda

1. Welcome and Introductions

2. What Is EIR?

3. What Is Coaching?

4. Coaching Demonstration

5. Demonstrate Practice Coaching with a Volunteer

6. Participants Practice Coaching

7. Discuss Participants' Role in EIR

8. Tips

9. Follow-Up Sessions

10. Questions, Concerns, and Thoughts

Figure 7-6 Coaching Training Agenda

Basic Elements of EIR

▸ Twenty minutes of daily supplemental reading instruction to small groups of six or seven struggling readers.

▸ Children receiving EIR participate in all of the regular reading instruction.

▸ Three-day cycle of reading and rereading narrative and informational books. Focus on attacking multisyllabic words, developing fluency, discussing vocabulary at point of contact in the story, practicing comprehension strategies, and engaging in high-level talk and writing about text.

▸ Teacher concentrates on coaching students in their use of reading strategies.

▸ Preparation for reading grade 3 EIR books to grade 1 children who need extra support in reading and also coaching these younger students as they read stories covered in grade 1 EIR lessons. If this cross-age tutoring is not in place, students work one day a week with an EIR partner instead.

▸ Transfer of EIR reading strategies to grade-level texts.

▸ Parent involvement.

Figure 7-7 Basic Elements of EIR

Next, describe coaching. Have participants read over Figure 7-8. Explain that coaching is giving children prompts, encouraging them, praising them as they attempt to figure out words on their own. Students have been learning a number of different strategies to figure out unknown words as they come to them. The purpose of coaching is to help children to learn to depend on themselves so they become good, independent readers. Show Figure 7-9 for prompts the coaches can use as they are working with the children.

To illustrate coaching show the following video clip:

Grade 3, Video 1 Teacher working with a group of grade 3 children

Conduct a coaching demonstration by modeling, with volunteer, and through partner practice. Model coaching by working through a story. Then, ask for a volunteer who will read another text as you coach. Finally, let people practice coaching with a partner by using a third text.

In conclusion, return to Figure 7-8 to review the coach's role. Also look at Figure 7-10, which provides tips for working with children. Ask for questions, thoughts, concerns. Schedule another session once the coaches have been working with children for 4 or 5 weeks.

Independent Coaching Role

▶ Work with one child at a time

▶ Classroom teacher gives you the book to use

▶ Child has a copy of the book

▶ Assist child in reading the book

▶ Reinforce strategies

▶ Give appropriate praise

Figure 7-8 Independent Coaching Role

Prompts for Teaching Children Decoding and Self-Monitoring Strategies for Multisyllabic Words

▶ Can you reread that? Did that make sense?

▶ You did a great job of figuring out that word. How did you do it?

▶ I like the way you self-corrected. How did you do that?

▶ Let's look at that word again. You said _____. Does that make sense (or look and sound right)?

Steps for Decoding Multisyllabic Words

▶ Break the word into chunks (approximate syllables) with one vowel (or vowel team) per chunk.

▶ Be flexible as you sound out the chunks, especially with the vowel sounds. If one sound doesn't work, try another.

▶ Remember to use context clues.

▶ After you sound out the chunks, try it again only faster.

▶ Remember that this will only get you close to the right word. Keep thinking of context.

Figure 7-9 Prompts for Teaching Children Decoding and Self-Monitoring Strategies for Multisyllabic Words

Figure 7-10 Tips for Working with Children

Summary

I cannot stress enough the importance of the ongoing professional learning experiences and the training of one-on-one coaches for students who need additional support in word recognition. While many believe these two components are extras, I have found that teachers who engage in professional learning experiences with colleagues feel especially successful and in turn their students are successful readers. Additionally, the one-on-one coaching may logistically be difficult to schedule, but it is imperative for struggling readers to receive as many opportunities as possible to practice and master reading with this much needed guided support.

It is my hope that this book, the companion *Catching Readers* books for other grades (Taylor, 2010a, 2010b, grades K and 4/5 forthcoming), and my book on school-based reading improvement (Taylor 2010c) will help you and your school help students learn to read well. It is my hope that this book has provided you with material that excites and motivates you to help students succeed. It is also my hope that this book has provided you with the information you need to implement EIR, either as an individual classroom teacher trying to improve your practice, or as part of a school improvement initiative. Should you have additional questions, go to the Heinemann website at www.heinemann.com for additional resources on EIR and search by Taylor or *Catching Readers*.

Finally, it is my hope that you are able to invest the time needed to understand and implement EIR in your classroom, because when you do, you will feel tremendous pride in what your students will accomplish, especially knowing you were instrumental in showing them they way. Thank you for the important work you do with and for children.

Works Cited

Adams, M. J. 1990. *Beginning to Read: Thinking and Learning About Print.* Cambridge, MA: MIT Press.

Anderson, N. A. 2007. *What Should I Read Aloud?* Newark, DE: International Reading Association.

Au, K. H. 2006. *Multicultural Issues and Literacy Achievement.* Mahwah, NJ: Lawrence Erlbaum.

Baumann, J. F., and E. J. Kame'enui. 2004. *Vocabulary Instruction: Research to Practice.* New York: Guilford.

Bear, D. R., M. Invernizzi, S. Templeton, and F. Johnston. 2007. *Words Their Way: Word Study for Phonics, Vocabulary, and Spelling Instruction.* 4th ed. Upper Saddle River, NJ: Pearson/Merrill Prentice Hall.

Beck, I. L. 2006. *Making Sense of Phonics: The Hows and Whys.* New York: Guilford.

Beck, I. L., M. G. McKeown, and L. Kucan. 2002. *Bringing Words to Life: Robust Vocabulary Instruction.* New York: Guilford.

Bergman, J. L. 1992. "SAIL—A Way to Success and Independence for Low-Achieving Readers." *The Reading Teacher* 45 (8): 598–602.

Blachowicz, C., and P. Fisher. 2000. "Vocabulary Instruction." In *Handbook of Reading Research, Volume III*, edited by M. L. Kamil, P. B. Mosenthal, P. D. Pearson, and R. Barr, 503–24. Mahwah, NJ: Lawrence Erlbaum.

———. 2002. *Teaching Vocabulary in All Classrooms.* 2d ed. Upper Saddle River, NJ: Pearson/Merrill Prentice Hall.

Bohn, C. M., A .D. Roehrig, and M. Pressley. 2004. "The First Days of School in the Classrooms of Two More Effective and Four Less Effective Primary-Grades Teachers." *The Elementary School Journal* 104: 271–87.

Brown, R., P. B. El-Dinary, M. Pressley, and L. Coy-Ogan. 1995. "A Transactional Strategies Approach to Reading Instruction." *The Reading Teacher* 49 (3): 256–57.

Chorzempa, B. F., and S. Graham. 2006. "Primary-Grade Teachers' Use of Within-Class Ability Grouping in Reading." *Journal of Educational Psychology* 98: 529–41.

Christensen, C. A., and J. A. Bowey. 2005. "The Efficacy of Orthographic Rime, Grapheme-Phoneme Correspondence, and Implicit Phonics Approaches to Teaching Decoding Skills." *Scientific Studies of Reading* 9: 327–49.

Clay, M. 1993. *Reading Recovery: A Guidebook for Teachers in Training.* Portsmouth, NH: Heinemann.

Connor, C. M., F. J. Morrison, and L. E. Katch. 2004. "Beyond the Reading Wars: Exploring the Effect of Child-Instruction Interactions on Growth in Early Reading." *Scientific Studies of Reading* 8: 305–36.

Consortium for Responsible School Change. 2005. *Description of Common Findings Across Multiple Studies on School Change in Reading.* University of Minnesota, Minnesota Center for Reading Research.

Cooney, B. 1982. *Miss Rumphius.* New York: Puffin.

Cunningham, P. M. 2009. *Phonics They Use: Words for Reading and Writing.* 5th ed. Boston: Pearson.

Cunningham, P. M., and D. R. Smith. 2008. *Beyond Retelling: Toward Higher Level Thinking and Big Ideas.* Newark DE: International Reading Association.

Day, J. P., D. L. Spiegel, J. McLellan, and V. B. Brown. 2002. *Moving Forward with Literature Circles.* New York: Scholastic.

Dolezal, S. E., L. M. Welsh, M. Pressley, and M. M. Vincent. 2003. "How Nine Third-Grade Teachers Motivate Student Academic Engagement." *Elementary School Journal* 103: 239–67.

Duke, N. K., and V. S. Bennett-Armistead. 2003. *Reading and Writing Informational Text in the Primary Grades: Research-Based Practices.* New York: Scholastic.

Edwards, P. A. 2004. *Children's Literacy Development: Making It Happen Through School, Family, and Community Involvement.* Boston: Pearson/Allyn & Bacon.

Foorman, B. R., C. Schatsneider, M. N. Eakin, J. M. Fletcher, L. C. Moats, and D. J. Francis. 2006. "The Impact of Instructional Practices in Grades 1 and 2 on Reading and Spelling Achievement in High Poverty Schools." *Contemporary Educational Psychology* 31: 1–29.

Foorman, B. R., and J. Torgesen. 2001. "Critical Elements of Classroom and Small-Group Instruction Promote Reading Success in All Children." *Learning Disabilities Research and Practice* 16: 203–12.

Fountas, I. C., and G. S. Pinnell. 1996. *Guided Reading: Good First Teaching for All Children.* Portsmouth, NH: Heinemann.

Fuchs, L. S., D. Fuchs, M. K. Hosp, and J. R. Jenkins. 2001. "Oral Reading Fluency as an Indicator of Reading Competence: A Theoretical, Empirical, and Historical Analysis." *Scientific Studies of Reading* 5: 239–56.

Gaetz, T. 1991. "The Effects of a Self-Monitoring Checklist on Elementary Students' Post-Reading Question-Answering Performance." Unpublished doctoral dissertation, University of Minnesota.

Galda, L., B. Cullinan, and L. Sipe. 2010. *Literature and the Child.* 7th ed. Belmont, CA: Thomson/Wadsworth.

Graves, M. F. 2007. "Conceptual and Empirical Bases for Providing Struggling Readers with Multifaceted and Long-Term Vocabulary Instruction." In *Effective Instruction for Struggling Readers K–6,* edited by B. M. Taylor and J. E. Ysseldyke, 55–83. New York: Teachers College Press.

Guthrie, J. T., A. Wigfield, P. Barbosa, K. C. Perencevich, A. Taboada, M.H. Davis, et al. 2004. "Increasing Reading Comprehension and Engagement Through Concept-Oriented Reading Instruction." *Journal of Educational Psychology* 96: 403–23.

Guthrie, J. T., and A. Wigfield, and C. VonSecker. 2000. "Effects of Integrated Instruction on Motivation and Strategy Use in Reading." *Journal of Educational Psychology* 92: 331–41.

Guzetti, B., ed. 2002. *Literacy in America: An Encyclopedia of History, Theory and Practice.* Santa Barbara, CA: ABE-CLIO.

Hadithi., M., A. Kennaway. 1990. *Lazy Lion.* London: Hodder and Stoughton.

Hamre, B. K., and R. C. Pianta. 2005. "Can Instructional and Emotional Support in the First-Grade Classroom Make a Difference for Children at Risk of School Failure?" *Child Development* 76 (5): 949–67.

Hasbrouck, J., and G. A. Tindal. 2006. "Oral Reading Fluency Norms: A Valuable Assessment Tool for Reading Teachers." *The Reading Teacher* 59 (7): 636–44.

Heffernan, L. 2004. *Critical Literacy and Writer's Workshop.* Newark, DE: International Reading Association.

Hiebert, E. H., and B. M. Taylor. 2000. "Beginning Reading Instruction: Research on Early Interventions." In *Handbook of Reading Research, Volume III,* edited by M. L. Kamil, P. B. Mosenthal, P. D. Pearson, and R. Barr, 455–82. Mahwah, NJ: Lawrence Erlbaum.

Hiebert, E. H., J. M. Colt, S. L. Catto, and E. C. Gury. 1992. "Reading and Writing of First-Grade Students in a Restructured Chapter I Program." *American Educational Research Journal* 29: 545–72.

John, J. L., and R. L. Berglund. 2005. *Fluency Strategies and Assessments.* Dubuque, IA: Kendall-Hunt.

Juel, C., and C. Minden-Cupp. 2000. "Learning to Read Words: Linguistic Units and Instructional Strategies." *Reading Research Quarterly* 35: 458–92.

Kelley, M. J., and N. Clausen-Grace. 2007. *Comprehension Shouldn't Be Silent.* Newark, DE: International Reading Association.

Kletsien, S. B., and M. J. Dreher. 2005. *Informational Text in K–3 Classrooms: Helping Children Read and Write.* Newark, DE: International Reading Association.

Klingner, J. K., S. Vaughn, M. E. Arguelles, M. T. Hughes, and S. A. Leftwich. 2004. Collaborative "Strategic Reading: Real World Lessons from Classroom Teachers." *Remedial and Special Education* 25: 291–302.

Knapp, M. S. 1995. *Teaching for Meaning in High-Poverty Classrooms.* New York: Teachers College Press.

Kuhn, M. R., and S. A. Stahl. 2003. "Fluency: A Review of Developmental and Remedial Practices." *Journal of Educational Psychology* 95: 3–21.

Lapp, D., D. Fisher, and T. D. Wolsey. 2009. *Literacy Growth for Every Child: Differentiated Small-Group Instruction, K–6.* New York: Guilford.

Leslie, L., and J. Caldwell. 2006. *Qualitative Reading Inventory 4.* Boston: Pearson.

Lipson, M. L., J. H. Mosenthal, J. Mekkelsen, and B. Russ. 2004. "Building Knowledge and Fashioning Success One School at a Time." *The Reading Teacher* 57 (6): 534–42.

Manning, M., G. Morrison, and D. Camp. 2009. *Creating the Best Literacy Block Ever.* New York: Scholastic.

Mathes, P. G., C. A. Denton, J. M. Fletcher, J. L. Anthony, D. J. Francis, and C. Schatschneider. 2005. "The Effects of Theoretically Different Instruction and Student Characteristics on the Skills of Struggling Readers." *Reading Research Quarterly* 40: 148–82.

McKeown, M. G., I. L. Beck, and R. G. K. Blake. 2009. "Rethinking Reading Comprehension Instruction: A Comparison of Instruction for Strategies and Content Approaches." *Reading Research Quarterly* 44 (3): 218–53.

National Reading Panel (NRP). 2000. *Teaching Children to Read: An Evidence-Based Assessment of the Scientific Research Literature on Reading and Its Implications for Reading Instruction.* Rockville, MD: National Institute for Child Health and Human Development, National Institutes of Health.

Oczkus, L. D. 2003. *Reciprocal Teaching at Work: Strategies for Improving Reading Comprehension.* Newark DE: International Reading Association.

Olness, R. 2007. *Using Literature to Enhance Content Area Instruction: A Guide for K–5 Teachers.* Newark, DE: International Reading Association.

Palincsar, A., and A. Brown. 1984. "Reciprocal Teaching of Comprehension-Fostering and Comprehension-Monitoring Activities." *Cognition and Instruction* 2: 117–75.

———. 1986. "Interactive Teaching to Promote Independent Learning from Text." *The Reading Teacher* 39 (8): 771–77.

Paratore, J. R., and R. L. McCormick, eds. 2007. *Classroom Literacy Assessment: Making Sense of What Students Know and Do.* New York: Guilford.

Pikulski, J. 1994. "Preventing Reading Failure: A Review of Five Effective Programs." *The Reading Teacher* 48: 30–39.

Pinnell, G., M. Fried, and R. Estice. 1990. "Reading Recovery: Learning How to Make a Difference." *The Reading Teacher* 90: 160–83.

Pressley, M. 2001. *Effective Beginning Reading Instruction: Executive Summary and Paper Commissioned by the National Reading Conference.* Chicago, IL: National Reading Conference.

———. 2006. *Reading Instruction That Works: The Case for Balanced Teaching.* 3d ed. New York: Guilford.

Pressley, M., S. E. Dolezal, L. M. Raphael, L. Mohan, A. D. Roehrig, and K. Bogner. 2003. *Motivating Primary-Grade Students.* New York: Guilford.

Pressley, M., P. B. El-Dinary, I. Gaskins, T. Schuder, J. L. Bergman, J. Almasi, and R. Brown. 1992. "Beyond Direct Explanation: Transactional Instruction of Reading Comprehension Strategies." *Elementary School Journal* 92: 511–54.

Pressley, M., L. Mohan, L. M. Raphael, and L. Fingeret. 2007. "How Does Bennett Woods Elementary School Produce Such High Reading and Writing Achievement?" *Journal of Educational Psychology* 99 (2): 221–40.

Raphael, T. E., K. Highfield, and K. H. Au. 2006. *QAR Now.* New York: Scholastic.

Raphael, T. E., L. S. Pardo, and K. Highfield. 2002. *Book Club: A Literature-Based Curriculum.* 2d ed. Lawrence, MA: Small Planet.

Rasinski, T. V. 2003. *The Fluent Reader: Oral Reading Strategies for Building Word Recognition, Fluency, and Comprehension.* New York: Scholastic.

Rosenshine, B., and Meister, C. 1994. "Reciprocal Teaching: A Review of the Research." *Review of Educational Research* 64 (4): 479–530.

Routman, R. 2008. *Teaching Essentials.* Portsmouth, NH: Heinemann.

Saunders, W. M., and C. Goldenberg. 1999. "Effects of Instructional Conversations and Literature Logs on Limited and Fluent English Proficient Students' Story Comprehension and Thematic Understanding." *The Elementary School Journal* 99: 279–301.

Seravallo, J. 2010. *Reading Instruction in Small Groups.* Portsmouth, NH: Heinemann.

Snow, C. E., M. S. Burns, and P. Griffin, eds. 1998. *Preventing Reading Difficulties in Young Children.* Washington, DC: National Academy.

Southall, M. 2009. *Differentiated Small-Group Reading Lessons.* New York: Scholastic.

Stahl, S. A. 2001. "Teaching Phonics and Phonemic Awareness." In *Handbook of Early Literacy Research,* edited by S.B. Neuman and D. Dickenson, 333–47. New York: Guilford.

Taberski, S. 2000. *On Solid Ground: Strategies for Teaching Reading K–3.* Portsmouth, NH: Heinemann.

Taylor, B. M. 1991. A Test of Phonemic Awareness for Classroom Use. www.earlyinterventioninreading.com.

———. 1998. "A Brief Review of Research on the Learning to Read Process." Minneapolis, MN: University of Minnesota.

———. 2001. "The Early Intervention in Reading Program: Research and Development Spanning Twelve Years." available at ww.earlyinterventionin-reading.com

———. 2010a. *Catching Readers, Grade 1.* Portsmouth, NH: Heinemann.

———. 2010b. *Catching Readers, Grade 2.* Portsmouth, NH: Heinemann.

———. 2010c. *Developing Successful, Engaged Readers K–8: A School-Based Professional Learning Model That Works.* Portsmouth, NH: Heinemann.

Taylor, B. M., G. E. Garcia, and P. D. Pearson. 2007. "Comprehension Strategies, High Level Talk About Text and Vocabulary: Effective Comprehension Instruction in Grades 2–5." Paper presented at the Research Conference, International Reading Association, Toronto, Canada.

Taylor, B. M., B. Hanson, K. J. Justice-Swanson, and S. Watts. 1997. "Helping Struggling Readers: Linking Small Group Intervention with Cross-Age Tutoring." *The Reading Teacher* 51: 196–209.

Taylor, B. M., L. Harris, P. D. Pearson, and G. E. Garcia. 1995. *Reading Difficulties: Instruction and Assessment.* 2d ed. New York: Random House.

Taylor, B. M., P. D. Pearson, K. Clark, and S. Walpole. 2000. "Effective Schools and Accomplished Teachers: Lessons About Primary Grade Reading Instruction in Low-Income Schools." *Elementary School Journal* 101 (2): 121–66.

Taylor, B. M., P. D. Pearson, D. S. Peterson, and M. C. Rodriguez. 2003. "Reading Growth in High-Poverty Classrooms: The Influence of Teacher Practices That Encourage Cognitive Engagement in Literacy Learning." *Elementary School Journal* 104: 3–28.

———. 2005. "The CIERA School Change Framework: An Evidence-Based Approach to Professional Development and School Reading Improvement." *Reading Research Quarterly* 40 (1): 40–69.

Taylor, B. M., D. S. Peterson, M. Marx, and M. Chein. 2007. "Scaling Up a Reading Reform in High-Poverty Elementary Schools." In *Effective Instruction for Struggling Readers, K–6*, edited by B. M. Taylor and J. E. Ysseldyke, 216–34. New York: Teachers College Press.

Taylor, B. M., D. S. Peterson, P. D. Pearson, and M. C. Rodriguez. 2002. "Looking Inside Classrooms: Reflecting on the 'How' as Well as the 'What' in Effective Reading Instruction." *The Reading Teacher* 56: 70–79.

Taylor, B. M., M. Pressley, and P. D. Pearson. 2002. "Research-Supported Characteristics of Teachers and Schools that Promote Reading Achievement." In *Teaching Reading: Effective Schools, Accomplished Teachers*, edited by B. M. Taylor and P. D. Pearson, 361–74. Mahwah, NJ: Erlbaum.

Taylor, B. M., Raphael, T. E., and Au, K. H. (in press). "Reading and School Reform." In *Handbook of Reading Research, Volume 4*, edited by M. Kamil, P. D. Pearson, P. Afflerbach, and E. Moje. London: Taylor & Francis.

Taylor, B. M., R. Short, B. Frye, and B. Shearer. 1992. "Classroom Teachers Prevent Reading Failure Among Low-Achieving First-Grade Students." *The Reading Teacher* 45: 592–97.

Valli, L., R. G. Croninger, and K. Walters. 2007. "Who (Else) Is the Teacher? Cautionary Notes on Teacher Accountability Systems." *American Journal of Education* 113: 635–62.

Van den Branden, K. 2000. "Does Negotiation of Meaning Promote Reading Comprehension? A Study of Multilingual Primary School Classes." *Reading Research Quarterly* 35: 426–43.

Walpole, S., and M. C. McKenna. 2009. *How to Plan Differentiated Reading Instruction: Resources for Grades K–3*. New York: Guilford.

Recommended Professional Readings

Resources on Phonemic Awareness

McCormick, C. E., R. N. Throneburg, and J. M. Smitley. 2002. *A Sound Start: Phonemic Awareness Lessons for Reading Success.* New York: Guilford.

Rog, L. J. 2001. *Early Literacy Instruction in Kindergarten.* Newark, DE: International Reading Association.

Resources on Phonics and Word-Recognition Instruction

Bear, D. R., M. Invernizzi., S. Templeton, and F. Johnston. 2007. *Words Their Way: Word Study for Phonics, Vocabulary, and Spelling Instruction*, 4th ed. Upper Saddle River, NJ: Pearson/Merrill Prentice Hall.

Beck, I. 2006. *Making Sense of Phonics: The Hows and Whys.* New York: Guilford.

Cunningham, P. 2009. *Phonics They Use: Words for Reading and Writing,* 5th ed. Boston: Pearson.

Carnine, D. W., J. Silbert, E .J. Kame'enui, and S.G. Tarver. 2004. *Direct Instruction Reading*, 4th edition. Upper Saddle River, NJ: Pearson.

Gaskins, I. W., L. C. Ehri, C. Cress, C. O'Hara, and D. Donnelly 1996. "Procedures for Word Learning: Making Discoveries About Words." *The Reading Teacher* 50: 312–27.

Taylor, B., R. Short, B. Frye, and B. Shearer. 1992. "Classroom Teachers Prevent Reading Failure Among Low-Achieving First–Grade Students." *The Reading Teacher* 45: 592–97.

Resources on Fluency

Johns, J. L., and R. L. Berglund. 2005. *Fluency Strategies and Assessments.* Dubuque, IA: Kendall-Hunt.

Rasinski, T. V. 2000. "Speed Does Matter in Reading." *The Reading Teacher* 54 (2): 146–51.

———. 2003. *The Fluent Reader: Oral Reading Strategies for Building Word Recognition, Fluency, and Comprehension.* New York: Scholastic.

Samuels, S. J., and A. Farstrup. eds. 2006. *What Research Has to Say About Fluency Instruction*, 3d ed. Newark, DE: International Reading Association.

Stahl, S. A. and M. R. Kuhn. 2002. "Making It Sound Like Language: Developing Fluency." *The Reading Teacher* 55 (6): 582–84.

Resources on Vocabulary

Bauman, J. F., and E. J. Kamen'eui (eds.). 2004. *Vocabulary Instruction: Research to Practice.* New York: Guilford.

Beck, I., M. McKeown, and L. Kucan. 2002. *Bringing Words to Life: Robust Vocabulary Instruction.* New York: Guilford.

Blachowicz, C., and P. Fisher. 2002. *Teaching Vocabulary in All Classrooms*, 2d ed. Upper Saddle River, NJ: Pearson/Merrill Prentice Hall.

Graves, M. F. 2007. "Conceptual and Empirical Bases for Providing Struggling Readers with Multifaceted and Long-Term Vocabulary Instruction." In *Effective Instruction for Struggling Readers K–6,* edited by B. M. Taylor and J. E. Ysseldyke, 55–83. New York: Teachers College Press.

Resources on Comprehension Strategies

Block, C., and M. Pressley. (Eds.). 2002. *Comprehension Strategies: Research-based Practices.* New York: Guilford.

Duke, N. K., and V. S. Bennett-Armistead. 2003. *Reading and Writing Informational Text in the Primary Grades.* New York: Scholastic.

Kelley, M. J., and N. Clausen-Grace. 2007. *Comprehension Shouldn't Be Silent.* Newark, DE: International Reading Association.

Kletsien, S. B., and M. J. Dreher. 2005. *Informational Text in K–3 Classrooms: Helping Children Read and Write.* Newark, DE: International Reading Association.

Klingner, J. K., S. Vaughan, M. E. Arguelles, M. T. Hughes, and S. A. Leftwich. 2004. "Collaborative Strategic Reading: Real World Lessons from Classroom Teachers." *Remedial and Special Education* 25: 291–302.

Raphael, T. E., K. Highfield, and K. H. Au. 2006. *QAR Now.* New York: Scholastic.

Resources on Comprehension: High-Level Talk and Writing About Text

Anderson, N. A. 2007. *What Should I Read Aloud?* Newark, DE: International Reading Association.

Cunningham, P. M. D. R. Smith. 2008. *Beyond Retelling: Toward Higher Level Thinking and Big Ideas.* Newark DE: International Reading Association..

Day, J. P., D. L. Spiegel, J. McLellan, and V. B. Brown. 2002. *Moving Forward with Literature Circles.* New York: Scholastic.

Galda, L., and B. Cullinan. 2010. *Literature and the Child*, 7th ed. Belmont, CA: Thomson/Wadsworth.

Kelley, M. J., and N. Clausen-Grace. 2007. *Comprehension Shouldn't Be Silent.* Newark, DE: International Reading Association.

Olness, R. 2007. *Using Literature to Enhance Content Area Instruction: A Guide for K–5 Teachers.* Newark, DE: International Reading Association.

Raphael, T. E., L. S. Pardo, and L. Highfield. 2002. *Book Club: A Literature-Based Curriculum.* 2d ed. Lawrence, MA: Small Planet.

Raphael, T. R., and S. McMahon. 1994. "Book Club: An Alternative Framework for Reading Instruction." *The Reading Teacher* 48 (2): 102–16.

Wood, K. D., N. L. Roser, and M. Martinez, M. 2001. "Collaborative Literacy: Lessons Learned from Literature." *The Reading Teacher* 55 (2): 102–11.

Resources on Balanced, Differentiated Instruction

Fountas, I. C., and G. S. Pinnell. 1996. *Guided Reading: Good First Teaching for All Children.* Portsmouth, NH: Heinemann.

Lapp, D., D. Fisher, and T. D. Wolsey. 2009. *Literacy Growth for Every Child: Differentiated Small-Group Instruction, K–6.* New York: Guilford.

Manning, M., G. Morrison, and D. Camp. 2009. *Creating the Best Literacy Block Ever.* New York: Scholastic.

Morrow, L. M. 2003. *Organizing and Managing the Language Arts Block: A Professional Development Guide.* New York: Guilford.

Pressley, M. 2006. *Reading Instruction That Works: The Case for Balanced Teaching,* 3d ed. New York: Guilford.

Routman, R. 2003 *Reading Essentials: The Specifics You Need to Teach Reading Well.* Portsmouth, NH: Heinemann.

———. 2008. *Teaching Essentials: Expecting the Most and Getting the Best from Every Learner, K–8.* Portsmouth, NH: Heinemann.

Serravallo, J. 2010. *Reading Instruction in Small Groups.* Portsmouth, NH: Heinemann.

Southall, M. 2009. *Differentiated Small-Group Reading Lessons.* New York: Scholastic.

Taberski, S. 2000. *On Solid Ground: Strategies for Teaching Reading K–3.* Portsmouth, NH: Heinemann.

Walpole, S., and M. C. McKenna. 2009. *How to Plan Differentiated Reading Instruction: Resources for Grades K–3.* New York: Guilford.

Resources on Support for Struggling Readers

Fuchs, D., L. Fuchs, and S. Vaughn (eds.). 2008. *Response to Intervention: An Overview for Educators.* Newark, DE: International Reading Association.

Gaskins, I. W. 2004. *Success with Struggling Readers: The Benchmark School Approach.* New York: Guilford.

McCormick, S. 2007. *Instructing Students Who Have Literacy Problems*, 5th ed. Upper Saddle River, NJ: Pearson.

Taylor, B. M. 2010a. *Catching Readers, Grade 1.* Portsmouth, NH: Heinemann.

———. 2010b. *Catching Readers, Grade 2.* Portsmouth, NH: Heinemann.

Tyner, B. 2009. *Small-Group Reading Instruction: A Differentiated Teaching Model for Beginning and Struggling Readers.* Newark, DE: International Reading Association.

Tyner, B., and S. E. Green. 2005. *Small-Group Reading Instruction: A Differentiated Teaching Model for Intermediate Grade Readers, Grades 3–8.* Newark, DE: International Reading Association.

Vaughn, S., J. Wanzek, and J. M. Fletcher. 2007. "Multiple Tiers of Intervention: A Framework for Prevention and Identification of Students with Reading/Learning Disabilities." In *Effective Instruction for Struggling Readers K–6,* edited by B. M. Taylor and J. E. Ysseldyke, 173–95. New York: Teachers College Press.

Resources on Motivating, Effective Pedagogy

Connor, C. M., F. J. Morrison, and L. E. Katch. 2004. "Beyond the Reading Wars: Exploring the Effect of Child-Instruction Interactions on Growth in Early Reading." *Scientific Studies of Reading* 8, 305–36.

Kelley, M. J., and N. Clausen-Grace. 2007. *Comprehension Shouldn't Be Silent.* Newark, DE: International Reading Association.

Manning, M., G. Morrison, and D. Camp. 2009. *Creating the Best Literacy Block Ever.* New York: Scholastic.

Olness, R. 2007. *Using Literature to Enhance Content-Area Instruction: A Guide for K–5 Teachers.* Newark, DE: International Reading Association.

Pressley, M. 2006. *Reading Instruction That Works: The Case for Balanced Teaching,* 3d ed. New York: Guilford.

Pressley, M., S. E. Dolezal, L. M. Raphael, L. Mohan, A. D. Roehrig, and K. Bogner. 2003. *Motivating Primary-Grade Students.* New York: Guilford.

Resources on Assessments

McKenna, M., and S. Stahl, S. 2003. *Assessment for Reading Instruction.* New York: Guilford.

Paratore, J. R., and R. L. McCormick (eds.). 2007. *Classroom Reading Assessment: Making Sense of What Students Know and Do.* New York: Guilford.

Pressley, M. 2006. *Reading Instruction That Works: The Case for Balanced Teaching,* 3d ed. New York: Guilford.

Taberski, S. 2000. *On Solid Ground: Strategies for Teaching Reading K–3.* Portsmouth, NH: Heinemann.

Resources on Culturally Responsive Instruction

Au, K. 2006. *Multicultural Issues and Literacy Achievement.* Mahwah, NJ: Erlbaum.

Gaitan, C. D. 2006. *Building Culturally Responsive Classrooms: A Guide for K–6 Teachers.* Thousand Oaks, CA: Corwin.

For a list and review of books for teachers on English language learners, see Opitz, M.F. and J. L. Harding-DeKam. 2007. "Teaching English-Language Learners." *The Reading Teacher* 60 (6): 590–93.

Resources on Schoolwide Reading Programs and Effective Schools

Allington, R. L., and S. A. Walmsley (Eds.). 2007. *No Quick Fix: Rethinking Literacy Programs in American's Elementary Schools* (RTI ed.). New York: Teachers College Press.

Morrow, L. M. 2003. *Organizing and Managing the Language Arts Block: A Professional Development Guide.* New York: Guilford.

Resnick, L. B., and S. Hampton 2009. "*Reading and Writing Grade by Grade, Revised Edition.* Newark, DE: International Reading Association and NCEE.

Reyes, P., J. D. Scribner, and A. P. Scribner (Eds.). 1999. *Lessons from High-Performing Hispanic Schools.* New York: Teachers College.

Taylor, B. M. 2010. *Developing Successful, Engaged Readers K–8: A School-Based Professional Learning Model That Works.* Portsmouth, NH: Heinemann.

Taylor, B. M., and P. D. Pearson (Eds.). 2002. *Teaching Reading: Effective Schools/Accomplished Teachers.* Mahwah, NJ: Erlbaum.

Taylor, B. M., D. S. Peterson, M. Marx, and M. Chein. 2007. "Scaling Up a Reading Framework for Prevention and Identification of Students with Reading/Learning Disabilities." In *Effective Instruction for Struggling Readers K–6,* edited by B. M. Taylor and J. E. Ysseldyke, 216–34. New York: Teachers College Press.

Taylor, B. M., T. E. Raphael, J. H. Au (in press.) "Reading anad School Reform." In *Handbook of Reading Research,* Volume IV. Edited b M. L. Kamil, P. D. Pearson, P. Afflerback, and E. Moje. London: Taylor & Francis.